KATHERINE AHARON

Daily Devotional for Women 2025

365 Devotions to Grow in Faith and Purpose

First edition

This book was professionally typeset on Reedsy.
Find out more at reedsy.com

Contents

Introduction

Life as a woman can be full of joys, challenges, and everything in between. Whether you are single, married, a mother, a professional, or all of the above, your days may feel like a whirlwind of responsibilities and emotions. In the midst of it all, it's easy to lose sight of the One who holds your heart and guides your steps. This 365-day devotional is a gentle reminder to pause, breathe, and reconnect with your Heavenly Father every single day.

Each day of this devotional is designed to meet you right where you are. With heartfelt reflections, meaningful scriptures, and practical applications, you'll discover encouragement to face daily challenges and wisdom to live in God's purpose. These devotions are not about perfection but about progress—an opportunity to grow closer to Christ as you walk through the seasons of life.

Through these pages, you will explore themes that speak to a woman's heart:

- **Trusting God in Uncertainty:** Learn to lean on His promises when life feels unstable.
- **Finding Strength in Weakness:** Discover how God's power can sustain you during your most vulnerable moments.
- **Embracing Your Worth:** See yourself as God sees you—loved, chosen, and redeemed.
- **Balancing Life and Faith:** Find encouragement to prioritize your spiritual life amid life's demands.

This journey isn't just about reading; it's about transformation. Take time to reflect, journal your thoughts, and pray through each day's devotion.

Whether you start your morning with these readings or end your evening meditating on them, let them draw you closer to the One who loves you unconditionally.

Dear sister, God has great plans for your life, and He is with you every step of the way. May these 365 days inspire you to live boldly in faith, resting in His promises and radiating His love.

I

January: Trusting God in New Beginnings

1

Embracing Change with Faith

January 1

"Jesus Christ is the same yesterday and today and forever." – Hebrews 13:8

In a world where change is constant, God's unchanging nature is a source of comfort and stability. Consider Jane, who had recently retired after 35 years in the same job. The transition was overwhelming. She felt unmoored without her usual routines and community. Yet, as she meditated on Hebrews 13:8, she was reminded that while her circumstances shifted, her foundation in Christ remained steady.

Life is full of changes—some planned, some unexpected. Jobs shift, relationships evolve, health fluctuates, and seasons of life come and go. It can feel unsettling when we face the unknown. But Hebrews 13:8 reassures us that while everything around us may change, Jesus remains the same. His love, promises, and character are unwavering.

Reflect on a recent change in your life. How did it impact your emotions and sense of security? Now consider how God has remained faithful through it all. While change can feel like a storm, God is your anchor, providing the strength and peace to weather it.

- Identify one area in your life where change has been difficult. Spend time journaling about how God's unchanging nature can bring you peace in this area. Find a verse that reminds you of His faithfulness and commit it to memory.

Prayer

Lord, thank You for being my constant in a world of change. Help me to trust in Your unchanging love and character as I navigate life's transitions. Amen.

January 2

Finding Purpose in Change

"And we know that in all things God works for the good of those who love him, who have been called according to his purpose."
Romans 8:28

When Clara's husband was offered a job in another state, she felt uprooted. Moving meant leaving behind her friends, church, and the community she'd built. As she unpacked boxes in her new home, she struggled to see how this change could be good. Then, she read Romans 8:28 and began praying for God to reveal His purpose. Over time, Clara found a new church, started volunteering, and formed meaningful relationships. What initially felt like loss turned into growth and new opportunities.

Change often disrupts our comfort zones, making it hard to see God's purpose in the moment. However, Romans 8:28 reminds us that God works all things for good for those who love Him. Even in the most challenging transitions, He weaves purpose into the process.

Are you facing a change that feels overwhelming or purposeless? Trust that God is at work, even if you can't see it yet. He may be leading you into new opportunities for growth, service, or deeper dependence on Him.

- Reflect on a past change that initially felt difficult but ultimately led to growth or blessing. Write down the lessons you learned and thank God for His faithfulness. Pray for clarity and patience as you look for purpose in your current situation.

Prayer

Lord, help me to trust that You are working for my good, even in the midst of change. Open my eyes to see Your purpose and guide me to embrace it with faith. Amen.

January 3

Letting Go of the Past

"Forget the former things; do not dwell on the past. See, I am doing a new thing! Now it springs up; do you not perceive it?"
Isaiah 43:18-19

After losing her job, Lisa found herself stuck in a loop of "what-ifs" and "if onlys." She clung to the security her old job had provided and couldn't imagine a future without it. Then, one day, she came across Isaiah 43:18-19. The verse challenged her to let go of the past and trust that God was doing something new. With time, Lisa began to see doors opening to opportunities she never would have pursued otherwise.

Clinging to the past can hinder us from embracing the new things God wants to do in our lives. Isaiah 43:18-19 reminds us not to dwell on what was but to focus on what God is creating. Change often requires us to release the old and trust that God's new plans are better.

What are you holding onto from the past? Whether it's a missed opportunity, a painful experience, or a season of comfort, ask God to help you release it so you can embrace the new thing He is doing.

- Write down something from the past that you need to let go of. Pray over it and then physically tear up the paper as a symbolic act of releasing it to God.

Prayer

Lord, help me to let go of the past and trust that You are doing a new thing in my life. Give me the courage to embrace the future with faith and hope. Amen.

January 4

Trusting God in the Unknown

"Trust in the Lord with all your heart and lean not on your own understanding; in all your ways submit to him, and he will make your paths straight."
Proverbs 3:5-6

Megan had always been a planner. She mapped out her life years in advance, but when her carefully crafted plans began to unravel—a breakup, an unexpected career change, and a family health crisis—she felt completely lost. It was during this season of uncertainty that she discovered Proverbs 3:5-6. As she meditated on the verse, Megan realized she was relying on her own understanding rather than trusting God with her future.

Life's uncertainties can be overwhelming, but God invites us to trust Him wholeheartedly. Proverbs 3:5-6 reminds us that while we may not always understand what's happening, God's perspective is far greater than ours. Trusting Him means submitting every decision, worry, and fear into His hands.

Think about the unknowns in your life right now. Are you clinging to control, or are you surrendering your plans to God? Trusting Him doesn't mean everything will become clear immediately, but it does mean that He will guide you step by step toward His perfect purpose.

- Make a list of the uncertainties you're facing. For each one, write a prayer of surrender, asking God to guide you. Post Proverbs 3:5-6 somewhere you'll see it daily as a reminder to trust Him.

Prayer

Lord, I surrender my plans, fears, and uncertainties to You. Help me to trust You with all my heart and lean on Your wisdom instead of my own. Thank You for making my paths straight as I follow You. Amen.

January 5

Finding Strength in Change

"I can do all this through him who gives me strength."
Philippians 4:13

Sarah's life had been turned upside down when she became a single mom. The weight of raising her children alone, balancing work, and managing finances felt unbearable. One evening, she broke down in tears, crying out to God for help. As she opened her Bible, she stumbled upon Philippians 4:13. This verse became her lifeline, reminding her that God's strength was sufficient for every challenge she faced.

Change can often leave us feeling weak, unprepared, or overwhelmed. But Philippians 4:13 reminds us that we're not alone in our struggles. Through Christ, we have access to divine strength that enables us to endure, adapt, and grow.

Whatever changes you're facing, remember that God's strength is made perfect in your weakness. Instead of trying to handle everything on your own, lean on Him. His power will sustain you through even the most difficult transitions.

- Identify a specific challenge you're facing due to change. Pray for God's strength to sustain you and take one proactive step toward addressing the challenge, trusting that He will provide what you need.

Prayer

Lord, I feel weak and overwhelmed, but I know Your strength is made perfect in my weakness. Help me to rely on You and trust that I can do all things through Christ who strengthens me. Amen.

January 6

Embracing New Beginnings

"Therefore, if anyone is in Christ, the new creation has come: The old has gone, the new is here!"

2 Corinthians 5:17

Mark had always resisted change. After decades in the same town, his family's decision to move left him feeling nostalgic and uncertain. As he packed his belongings, he stumbled across an old journal filled with memories of how God had worked in his life. The reminder of God's faithfulness sparked hope in his heart, and 2 Corinthians 5:17 became his anthem: God was doing something new.

Change is often God's way of ushering in new beginnings. Just as we are made new in Christ, life's transitions can open doors to growth, opportunities, and deeper faith. Embracing change requires letting go of the past and trusting God to lead us into what's next.

Is there a new beginning God is calling you to embrace? It might feel uncomfortable or uncertain, but trust that His plans for you are good and purposeful.

- Take one step toward embracing a new beginning in your life, whether it's pursuing a new opportunity, joining a community, or starting a new habit. Reflect on how God's work in your past prepares you for this new season.

Prayer

Lord, thank You for making all things new. Help me to embrace the changes You bring into my life and to trust that they are part of Your good plan. Lead me into this new season with faith and joy. Amen.

January 7

Growing Through Change

"Consider it pure joy, my brothers and sisters, whenever you face trials of many kinds, because you know that the testing of your faith produces perseverance."

James 1:2-3

When David lost his job, he initially saw it as a setback. But over time, he realized it was an opportunity for growth. He pursued a new career path, strengthened his relationship with God, and developed perseverance he never thought possible. Looking back, he saw how the trial had shaped him into a stronger, more faithful person.

James 1:2-3 encourages us to view challenges as opportunities for growth. Change often tests our faith, but it also deepens it. Just as muscles grow stronger through resistance, our spiritual lives are strengthened through trials.

Are you facing a change that feels more like a trial? Instead of resisting it, ask God what He wants to teach you through the process. Embrace the opportunity to grow in faith, perseverance, and character.

- Write down one lesson God is teaching you through a current or past change. Pray for a heart that seeks growth instead of comfort, and look for ways to apply this lesson in your daily life.

Prayer

Lord, thank You for using change to grow my faith and perseverance. Help me to see trials as opportunities to deepen my trust in You and to embrace the growth You bring through them. Amen.

2

Surrendering Your Fears

J**anuary 8**

Facing Fear with Faith

"The Lord is my light and my salvation—whom shall I fear? The Lord is the stronghold of my life—of whom shall I be afraid?"

Psalm 27:1

Fear is a universal human emotion. It can range from small worries to overwhelming anxiety that paralyzes us. But Psalm 27:1 reminds us of a powerful truth: when God is our light and salvation, fear loses its grip. David, the psalmist, faced countless threats, yet he boldly declared that he would not be afraid because he trusted in God's protection and strength.

Faith doesn't mean the absence of fear; it means choosing to believe in God's power over your fear. When fear arises, it's often rooted in a lack of control or uncertainty about the future. But God is sovereign, and nothing escapes His knowledge or authority. He invites you to place your fears in His hands and trust in His goodness.

What fears are you holding onto today? Maybe it's fear of failure, rejection, or loss. Acknowledge these fears and remind yourself that God is bigger than anything you face. Fear can feel overwhelming, but faith acts as a shield, helping us to move forward with confidence.

- Write down your top three fears and pray over each one, surrendering them to God. Keep Psalm 27:1 nearby as a reminder of God's presence and power. Commit to speaking this verse aloud whenever fear starts to creep in.

Prayer

Lord, You are my light and my salvation. I surrender my fears to You, knowing that You are stronger than anything I face. Help me to trust You more deeply and walk in faith each day. Amen.

January 9

God Is Bigger Than Your Fears

"So do not fear, for I am with you; do not be dismayed, for I am your God. I will strengthen you and help you; I will uphold you with my righteous right hand."
Isaiah 41:10

Fear often magnifies our problems, making them seem larger than they are. But when we focus on God instead of our fears, we gain perspective. Isaiah 41:10 is a powerful reminder that God's presence and strength are always available to us. He promises to uphold us with His righteous right hand, a symbol of His authority and care.

When fear threatens to overwhelm you, remember who God is. He is omnipotent, omnipresent, and omniscient. He knows your struggles and is more than capable of handling them. This doesn't mean challenges will disappear instantly, but it does mean you can face them with courage, knowing that God is by your side.

What fears have you allowed to take center stage in your life? Perhaps it's fear of the unknown, fear of change, or fear of inadequacy. Take time today to shift your focus from your fears to God's greatness.

- Make a list of attributes that describe God, such as "faithful," "all-powerful," and "loving." Whenever fear arises, meditate on these attributes and thank God for His character.

Prayer

Lord, thank You for being greater than my fears. Help me to focus on Your power and faithfulness instead of my anxieties. Strengthen me as I trust in Your promises. Amen.

January 10

Perfect Love Casts Out Fear

"There is no fear in love. But perfect love drives out fear, because fear has to do with punishment."

1 John 4:18

Fear often stems from a sense of punishment, failure, or rejection. But God's love is perfect, and His perfect love casts out all fear. When you truly understand and accept God's love for you, fear loses its hold.

God's love isn't conditional or based on your performance. It is steadfast and unchanging. Fear tries to tell you that you're not enough or that something bad is inevitable, but God's love reminds you that you are His beloved child, and nothing can separate you from Him.

Are you struggling to trust in God's love? Fear grows when we doubt His goodness or believe the lies of the enemy. Spend time meditating on His love today and let it push fear out of your heart.

- Write a letter to God expressing your fears. Then, write down verses about God's love, like Romans 8:38-39. Meditate on these verses and ask God to help you feel secure in His love.

Prayer

Father, thank You for Your perfect love that drives out fear. Help me to trust in Your love and rest in the assurance that I am fully known and fully loved by You. Amen.

January 11
Surrendering the Fear of Failure
"Commit to the Lord whatever you do, and he will establish your plans."
Proverbs 16:3

The fear of failure can stop us from pursuing our God-given dreams. But Proverbs 16:3 reminds us that when we commit our plans to the Lord, He establishes them. This doesn't mean everything will always go according to our expectations, but it does mean God will guide us toward His purposes.

Failure isn't the end—it's an opportunity to grow and trust God more deeply. When you surrender your fear of failure to Him, you open yourself up to His direction and provision.

What steps have you been avoiding because of the fear of failure? Remember, your worth isn't defined by your successes or mistakes but by your identity in Christ.

- Take one small step toward a goal you've been avoiding. Trust God with the outcome and remind yourself that He is working through every situation.

Prayer
Lord, I surrender my fear of failure to You. Help me to trust that You are in control and that You will guide my steps according to Your will. Amen.

January 12
Surrendering the Fear of the Unknown
"Trust in the Lord with all your heart and lean not on your own understanding;
in all your ways submit to him, and he will make your paths straight."
Proverbs 3:5-6

The fear of the unknown is one of the most challenging fears to surrender. We often want to have all the answers before moving forward, but Proverbs

3:5-6 calls us to trust in God's wisdom rather than our own. When we try to control every detail of our lives, we limit our ability to experience the fullness of God's guidance.

God's promise is clear: if we trust Him and submit our ways to Him, He will make our paths straight. This doesn't mean life will be without challenges, but it does mean that He will lead us in the direction of His perfect plan. Trusting God with the unknown requires faith, patience, and surrender.

What uncertainties are causing you anxiety right now? Whether it's a career decision, a relationship, or a health concern, God knows the outcome and has already gone before you. Surrendering the fear of the unknown allows you to rest in His sovereignty.

- Write down one area of your life where you feel uncertain. Pray specifically over this area, asking God to guide your steps. Then, take a practical step forward, even if it's small, trusting that God will reveal the next step in His timing.

Prayer

Father, I surrender my fear of the unknown to You. Help me to trust Your wisdom and guidance, even when I can't see the full picture. Lead me on the path You have prepared for me. Amen.

January 13

Surrendering the Fear of Rejection

"Am I now trying to win the approval of human beings, or of God? Or am I trying to please people? If I were still trying to please people, I would not be a servant of Christ."
Galatians 1:10

The fear of rejection can be crippling, causing us to seek approval from others instead of focusing on God's opinion of us. Galatians 1:10 reminds us that our primary goal should be to please God, not people. When we base our worth on human acceptance, we set ourselves up for disappointment. But when we root our identity in Christ, we can live confidently, knowing we are fully accepted and loved by Him.

Rejection is an inevitable part of life, but it doesn't define your value. Jesus Himself faced rejection, yet He remained faithful to God's calling. In the same way, God calls you to trust in His approval and let go of the need to please everyone around you.

Are there areas where the fear of rejection is holding you back? Perhaps it's preventing you from sharing your faith, pursuing a dream, or building meaningful relationships. Reflect on how God's acceptance frees you to live boldly.

- Make a list of truths about your identity in Christ, such as "I am loved," "I am chosen," and "I am enough." Refer to this list whenever you feel insecure or rejected. Take one step today to act boldly in an area where you've been held back by fear of rejection.

Prayer

Lord, help me to surrender my fear of rejection and focus on Your approval. Remind me that my worth is found in You alone, and give me the courage to live boldly for You. Amen.

January 14

Walking in Freedom from Fear

"For God has not given us a spirit of fear, but of power and of love and of a sound mind."

2 Timothy 1:7

Fear is not from God. He has given you a spirit of power, love, and a sound mind—tools to help you live fearlessly and confidently in Him. Walking in freedom from fear means not allowing it to control your decisions, emotions, or identity.

To overcome fear, you must replace it with faith. This requires daily surrender, constant prayer, and a focus on God's promises. When you feel fear rising, remind yourself that you have the power of the Holy Spirit within you. Fear may still knock at the door of your heart, but you don't have to let it in.

As you reflect on this week, consider how surrendering your fears has allowed you to grow in faith and trust. Fear may not disappear completely, but as you walk closely with God, it loses its hold over you.

- Identify one fear that has consistently held you back. Write down a declaration of faith, such as "I will not fear because God is with me" or "I am walking in freedom through Christ." Speak this declaration out loud each day this week as a reminder of the truth.
- Spend time in prayer, thanking God for the freedom He has given you and asking Him to help you continue walking in that freedom.

Prayer

Father, thank You for the spirit of power, love, and a sound mind. I declare that I am free from fear because of Your presence in my life. Help me to walk boldly in faith, trusting You in every area. Amen.

3

God's Guidance in Uncertainty

January 15

Trusting God's Plan

"'For I know the plans I have for you,' declares the Lord, 'plans to prosper you and not to harm you, plans to give you hope and a future.'"

Jeremiah 29:11

Imagine a hiker lost in the forest. They hold a map in their hands but have no idea how to use it. Then, a guide arrives, offering to lead them to safety. The hiker must decide: trust the guide or try to figure it out alone. This is often our experience with God's guidance.

Jeremiah 29:11 is one of the most comforting verses in Scripture. It reminds us that God has a plan for us—a plan to give us hope and a future. But what happens when we can't see the plan? When uncertainty clouds our vision, trusting in God's unseen plan becomes both a challenge and a necessity.

The Israelites were in exile when God spoke these words to them. They likely felt abandoned and hopeless, but God reassured them that His plans were good, even if they couldn't see the full picture yet. In the same way, God's guidance may not always be immediately clear, but His promises remain steadfast.

What uncertainties are you facing today? Perhaps you're waiting for clarity on a job, a relationship, or a major life decision. God invites you to trust Him, even when the path ahead is unclear. Remember, He sees the beginning and the end of your story, and His plans are always for your good.

- Take a moment to reflect on a time when God guided you in the past. Write it down as a reminder of His faithfulness. Then, pray and surrender your current uncertainties to Him, asking for His guidance and peace.

Prayer

Lord, thank You for having a plan for my life. Even when I can't see what's ahead, help me to trust that Your plans are good. Lead me with Your wisdom and peace. Amen.

January 16

God's Word as a Lamp

"Your word is a lamp to my feet and a light to my path."
Psalm 119:105

Picture yourself walking through a dark tunnel with a small lantern in your hand. The light doesn't illuminate the entire path, but it provides just enough visibility to take the next step. This is how God's Word operates in our lives. It may not reveal the entire journey, but it gives us clarity for the steps we need to take today.

Psalm 119:105 reminds us that Scripture is our guiding light. When life feels uncertain, God's Word offers wisdom, comfort, and direction. Consider a man named James who was unsure about taking a new job in a different city. Overwhelmed by the decision, he prayed and immersed himself in Scripture. While reading Proverbs 3:5-6, he felt God's peace about moving forward. Though he didn't know what the future held, God's Word gave him the confidence to take the first step.

If you're feeling lost or uncertain, let God's Word be your anchor. Open your Bible and seek His truth. You may not receive a clear answer immediately, but Scripture will always guide you toward God's will.

- Spend 15 minutes today reading a chapter from Proverbs or Psalms. Highlight any verses that stand out to you and reflect on how they apply to your current situation. Write one verse down and carry it with you throughout the week.

Prayer

Lord, thank You for Your Word, which lights my path in times of uncertainty. Help me to seek Your truth daily and trust in the guidance You provide. Amen.

January 17

God Goes Before You

"The Lord himself goes before you and will be with you; he will never leave you nor forsake you. Do not be afraid; do not be discouraged."
Deuteronomy 31:8

Think about the courage it takes for a child to jump into a pool for the first time. What makes them take the leap? The reassurance that their parent is in the water, ready to catch them. This is the kind of confidence we can have in God, who goes before us in every situation.

Moses spoke these words to Joshua as he prepared to lead the Israelites into the Promised Land. The journey ahead was filled with uncertainty, but God's promise was clear: He would go before them and never leave them. In the same way, God is already in the future, preparing the way for you.

Are you afraid to take a step forward because of the unknown? Remember, God is not only with you—He is ahead of you. Like a trailblazer clearing the path, He removes obstacles and ensures that His plans for you come to fruition. Trust that He has already prepared what lies ahead.

- Identify one area of your life where you need to move forward despite uncertainty. Take a small step in faith today, trusting that God has already gone before you.

Prayer

Lord, thank You for going before me and preparing the way. Help me to walk forward in faith, knowing that You will never leave me nor forsake me. Amen.

January 18

Waiting on God's Timing

"But those who wait on the Lord shall renew their strength; they shall mount up with wings like eagles, they shall run and not be weary, they shall walk and not faint."

Isaiah 40:31

Have you ever planted a seed and waited impatiently for it to sprout? Even though you can't see it, there's life beneath the soil. In the same way, God is often working in unseen ways while we wait. Waiting is one of the most challenging aspects of faith because it requires surrendering control and trusting in God's perfect timing.

Consider Sarah in the Bible, who waited years for the fulfillment of God's promise of a son. Though her faith wavered at times, God remained faithful. Sarah's story reminds us that God's timing is always better than our own.

In seasons of uncertainty, waiting can feel unbearable. You may wonder why God hasn't answered your prayers yet. But Isaiah 40:31 assures us that waiting on the Lord renews our strength. Instead of rushing ahead or growing discouraged, we are called to rest in the knowledge that God is working behind the scenes for our good.

If you're waiting on God for clarity, direction, or provision, trust that He sees the bigger picture. His timing is never late, and His plans are worth the wait.

- Spend 10 minutes in silence today, reflecting on God's faithfulness in your past seasons of waiting. Journal how He came through for you and how you can trust Him in your current situation.

Prayer

Lord, waiting is hard, but I trust in Your perfect timing. Renew my strength and help me to remain patient and faithful as You work all things together for good. Amen.

January 19

Listening for God's Voice

"Whether you turn to the right or to the left, your ears will hear a voice behind you, saying, 'This is the way; walk in it.'"

Isaiah 30:21

Imagine standing at a crossroads, unsure which path to take. Then, a calm voice speaks, guiding you toward the right direction. This is how God works in our lives—He speaks to us in the midst of our uncertainty.

In Isaiah 30:21, God promises to guide His people, even when they face difficult decisions. However, listening for God's voice requires stillness and attentiveness. In a world full of noise and distractions, it can be easy to miss His gentle whisper.

Consider the story of Elijah in 1 Kings 19. God didn't speak to Elijah through a powerful wind, earthquake, or fire, but in a gentle whisper. This teaches us that God often speaks in subtle ways, and we must quiet our hearts to hear Him.

Are you seeking God's guidance today? Take time to pause, pray, and listen. His voice may come through Scripture, prayer, a trusted friend, or even a sense of peace in your heart.

- Set aside 15 minutes today to sit quietly with God. Pray for clarity and then listen. Write down any thoughts, Scriptures, or impressions you feel during this time.

Prayer

Lord, help me to quiet my heart and listen for Your voice. Guide me in the decisions I face and lead me on the path You have prepared for me. Amen.

January 20

Following God's Direction

"Commit your way to the Lord; trust in Him, and He will act."
Psalm 37:5

Imagine a sailor navigating uncharted waters with a compass. The sailor doesn't rely on their instincts alone but trusts the compass to guide them. Similarly, God's direction is like a compass for our lives, and we must trust Him to lead us, even when the way seems uncertain.

Psalm 37:5 is a call to action: commit your way to the Lord and trust Him to act. Following God's direction often requires faith and obedience, even when His plans differ from ours. Take Jonah, for example. Initially, he resisted God's call to go to Nineveh, but when he finally obeyed, he witnessed God's power and mercy in an incredible way.

If you're at a crossroads, ask yourself: Are you willing to follow God's direction, even if it takes you out of your comfort zone? Trusting Him doesn't mean the journey will be easy, but it does mean it will be purposeful.

- Identify one area where you've been hesitant to follow God's direction. Take a step of obedience today, no matter how small, and trust God with the outcome.

Prayer

Lord, I commit my way to You. Help me to trust Your direction and follow where You lead, even when the path is unclear. Strengthen my faith as I step out in obedience. Amen.

January 21

Resting in God's Sovereignty

"Be still, and know that I am God."
Psalm 46:10

Picture a stormy sea with waves crashing and winds roaring. In the middle of the chaos, a ship's captain drops anchor, knowing it will keep them steady. In the same way, God calls us to rest in His sovereignty, even when life feels turbulent.

Psalm 46:10 is a powerful reminder to pause and acknowledge God's control. Being still doesn't mean inactivity; it means surrendering your striving and trusting that God is in control. Consider the disciples in Mark 4, panicking during a storm while Jesus slept in the boat. When they woke Him, Jesus calmed the storm with a word, demonstrating His power over every situation.

Life is filled with uncertainties, but God is never surprised. He is sovereign over every detail of your life, and His plans are perfect. Resting in His sovereignty allows you to find peace, even in the midst of chaos.

- Take a Sabbath moment today. Spend 20 minutes in stillness, reflecting on God's sovereignty. Thank Him for being in control, even when life feels uncertain.

Prayer

Lord, I surrender my worries and uncertainties to You. Help me to rest in Your sovereignty and trust that You are in control of every situation. Calm my heart and fill me with Your peace. Amen.

4

Renewing Your Mind for a Fresh Start

January 22

Letting Go of the Old

"Forget the former things; do not dwell on the past. See, I am doing a new thing!"

Isaiah 43:18-19

Starting fresh with God often begins with letting go of the past. This may include past mistakes, painful memories, missed opportunities, or even successes we cling to. When we hold tightly to what's behind us, it becomes difficult to embrace the new thing God is doing. Letting go doesn't mean forgetting completely or pretending something didn't happen—it means choosing to trust God with those experiences and refusing to let them define us.

Isaiah reminds us that God is always at work, creating new opportunities and pathways. When He says, "I am doing a new thing," it's an invitation to step forward in faith and release what's no longer beneficial. Holding onto past hurts or regrets can weigh us down, but when we let go, we make room for God to work in new and unexpected ways. What are you still holding onto that might be hindering the fresh start God wants to give you?

- Spend time journaling about what you feel is holding you back. Identify one or two specific things from your past—whether it's an event, a failure, or a fear. Write a prayer of surrender for each, asking God to help you release it. Then, write down a verse, such as Isaiah 43:18-19, and meditate on it throughout the day.
- For a symbolic act, consider writing what you need to let go of on a piece of paper. Pray over it, and then either tear it up or place it in a "God box," symbolizing that you are giving it to Him.

Prayer

Father, thank You for Your promise to do something new in my life. Help me to let go of the things that are holding me back, and trust You fully for the fresh start You are leading me into. Amen.

January 23

Trusting God's Plan

"For I know the plans I have for you,' declares the Lord, 'plans to prosper you and not to harm you, plans to give you hope and a future.'"
Jeremiah 29:11

Trusting God's plan isn't always easy, especially when life takes unexpected turns. Yet Jeremiah 29:11 reminds us that God's plans for us are good. Even when we don't understand His timing or methods, we can rest assured that His intentions are to bring us hope and a future.

In seasons of transition or fresh starts, it's tempting to take control and try to force outcomes. But trusting God means surrendering your plans to Him, knowing that His ways are higher than yours. When you're faced with uncertainty or doubt, lean into the truth of His Word. God's plan is not just about your immediate circumstances but about His eternal purposes for your life.

What part of your life are you struggling to trust God with? Maybe it's a career decision, a relationship, or a financial issue. Reflect on how you can shift your focus from worrying about outcomes to trusting God with the process.

- Choose an area of your life where you've been trying to control the outcome. Take time to surrender that specific situation to God in prayer. Write down Jeremiah 29:11 and place it somewhere visible, like a mirror or refrigerator, as a reminder to trust Him daily.
- Commit to praying each morning for God's will to be done, and resist the urge to take matters into your own hands. Instead, practice patience and gratitude, trusting that God's timing is perfect.

Prayer

Lord, I thank You that Your plans for me are good. Help me to trust You in every area of my life, especially when things don't make sense. Give me the strength to surrender my desires and follow Your lead. Amen.

January 24

Overcoming Fear of the Unknown

"So do not fear, for I am with you; do not be dismayed, for I am your God. I will strengthen you and help you; I will uphold you with my righteous right hand."
Isaiah 41:10

Fear of the unknown can often paralyze us when we face new beginnings. What if things don't work out? What if the path ahead is too difficult? These questions can swirl in our minds, leaving us hesitant to take the steps God is calling us to. However, Isaiah 41:10 reminds us that fear has no place in our walk with God because He is always with us.

God doesn't promise that the road ahead will always be smooth, but He does promise His presence, strength, and guidance. His righteous right hand symbolizes His power and ability to protect and sustain us through any challenges. When fear arises, it's important to confront it with the truth of God's Word. The same God who created the universe walks with you through every uncertainty.

Reflect on the fears that may be holding you back from fully trusting God for a fresh start. Are you afraid of failure, rejection, or stepping out of your comfort zone? Take time to identify these fears and bring them before the Lord, remembering His promise to uphold you.

Prayer

Lord, thank You for walking with me in every season of my life. When fear arises, remind me of Your constant presence and unchanging power. Help me to trust You and step forward in faith. Amen.

January 25

Renewing Your Mind

"Do not conform to the pattern of this world, but be transformed by the renewing of your mind. Then you will be able to test and approve what God's will is—his good, pleasing and perfect will."

Romans 12:2

A fresh start requires a fresh perspective, and that begins with renewing your mind. The world often tells us to focus on worry, fear, and self-reliance, but God's Word calls us to transform our thinking by aligning it with His truth. Renewing your mind allows you to see situations through God's eyes and discern His will for your life.

When your thoughts are filled with doubt or negativity, they can become a barrier to fully trusting God. The process of renewal isn't a one-time event but a daily practice of immersing yourself in Scripture, prayer, and worship. As you fill your mind with God's truth, you'll find it easier to let go of limiting beliefs and embrace His promises.

What thoughts or mindsets do you need to let go of today? Maybe it's the idea that you're not good enough, or perhaps it's a fear of failure. Take these thoughts captive and replace them with God's promises.

• Spend 15 minutes in God's Word, focusing on a passage that speaks to your current situation. Write down one verse that stands out to you and meditate on it throughout the day.

• When negative or fearful thoughts arise, pause and replace them with God's truth. For example, if you're worried about the future, remind yourself of Jeremiah 29:11, which declares God's good plans for your life.

Prayer

Lord, transform my mind and help me focus on Your truth. Teach me to release negative thoughts and replace them with Your promises. Renew my perspective so that I may walk in confidence and peace. Amen.

January 26

Taking the First Step

"The Lord makes firm the steps of the one who delights in him."
Psalm 37:23

Trusting God often requires action. While it's important to pray and seek His guidance, there comes a time when you must take the first step of faith. Even small steps of obedience demonstrate your trust in God's ability to guide and sustain you.

Psalm 37:23 reminds us that when we delight in the Lord—when our hearts are aligned with His will—He establishes our steps. This doesn't mean the journey will always be easy, but it does mean that God will provide the strength and wisdom you need along the way.

Think about what God might be calling you to do. Is there a step you've been hesitant to take because of fear or uncertainty? Remember, it's not about having the entire plan figured out—it's about trusting the One who holds your future.

• Identify one step you can take toward a fresh start. This might involve starting a new project, reaching out to someone for reconciliation, or committing to a daily habit of prayer or Bible study.

- Take that step today, trusting that God will guide you. If you feel unsure, pause to pray and ask for His direction before moving forward.

Prayer

Lord, help me to take the steps You are calling me to, even when I feel uncertain. Strengthen my faith and guide my path so that I may walk in obedience and confidence. Amen.

January 27

God's Strength in Your Weakness

"But he said to me, 'My grace is sufficient for you, for my power is made perfect in weakness.'"
2 Corinthians 12:9

Starting fresh can feel overwhelming, especially when you feel inadequate or unprepared. But God's promise is clear: His grace is sufficient, and His power is made perfect in your weakness.

This truth is freeing because it reminds us that we don't have to rely on our own strength. Instead, we can depend on God's grace to sustain us and His power to work through us. Your weaknesses are not limitations—they're opportunities for God to demonstrate His glory.

- Reflect on an area where you feel weak or inadequate. Write a prayer asking for God's strength in that specific area. Then, look for ways to rely on His power rather than your own efforts.

Prayer

Lord, thank You for Your grace that strengthens me in my weakness. Remind me to depend on You daily and trust in Your power. Amen.

January 28

Trusting God Completely

"Blessed is the one who trusts in the Lord, whose confidence is in him."
Jeremiah 17:7

Complete trust in God is not just about specific moments—it's a lifestyle. It means placing your confidence in Him, not just when things are going well but also in the uncertainties and challenges of life.

As you reflect on this week, consider where you've grown in trusting God. Are there areas where you still hesitate? Trusting God completely brings peace and blessings, as you learn to rely on His wisdom and love.

- Spend time journaling about how you've experienced God's faithfulness this week. Identify one area where you want to grow in trust and commit it to prayer.

Prayer

Father, I place my full trust in You. Teach me to walk in confidence and faith, knowing that You are always faithful. Amen.

II

February: Love, Relationships, and Grace

5

Loving Others as Christ Loves You

F ebruary 1
The Measure of Love
"A new command I give you: Love one another. As I have loved you, so you must love one another."
John 13:34

Jesus spoke these words to His disciples shortly before His crucifixion. It wasn't just a suggestion—it was a command. He didn't simply say to love one another; He raised the standard by instructing us to love as He loves. That's a sacrificial, unconditional, and selfless love.

Think of Maria, a woman who tirelessly cared for her aging mother. She sacrificed her time, resources, and personal comfort to ensure her mother felt loved. Though it was difficult, Maria found strength in reflecting on how Jesus demonstrated His love through sacrifice. His love for us isn't based on convenience or worthiness—it's a choice and commitment.

We often love people conditionally, based on how they treat us or what we receive in return. But Jesus calls us to a higher standard. He loved even those who betrayed, abandoned, and crucified Him. His love is patient, kind, and forgiving, and He invites us to love others in the same way.

- Identify one person in your life who needs to feel Christ-like love. Do something intentional to show them love today, whether it's through a kind word, an act of service, or forgiving them for a past wrong.

Prayer

Lord, thank You for loving me unconditionally. Help me to love others as You love me. Teach me to be patient, forgiving, and selfless in my relationships. Amen.

February 2

Loving the Unlovable

"But I tell you, love your enemies and pray for those who persecute you."
Matthew 5:44

Jason's coworker, Mike, was constantly critical of him, spreading gossip and making work difficult. Jason's initial reaction was anger and resentment. But during a church service, he heard a sermon on Matthew 5:44, and it challenged him to see Mike through Christ's eyes. Instead of retaliating, Jason began praying for Mike. Over time, his heart softened, and his kindness began to break down the walls between them.

Loving our enemies goes against our natural instincts, but Jesus calls us to a higher standard. When we choose to love those who are difficult or hurtful, we reflect God's character. After all, God loved us even while we were still sinners (Romans 5:8).

Loving the unlovable doesn't mean tolerating abuse or toxic behavior. It means showing them grace, praying for their well-being, and choosing forgiveness over bitterness.

- Think of someone who has hurt or wronged you. Take a moment to pray for them today. Ask God to help you see them through His eyes and to give you the strength to show them kindness and forgiveness.

Prayer

Lord, it's hard to love those who hurt me, but I know You call me to reflect Your grace. Help me to love and pray for my enemies, trusting You to work in their hearts and mine. Amen.

February 3

Love in Action

"Dear children, let us not love with words or speech but with actions and in truth."

1 John 3:18

When Laura heard that her neighbor, Mrs. Green, had fallen ill, she decided to bake a meal and visit her. Mrs. Green was touched by the gesture, and their relationship grew stronger. Laura's simple act of kindness was a tangible expression of love that made a lasting impact.

Love isn't just something we say—it's something we do. 1 John 3:18 reminds us that real love is active, not passive. It's easy to say, "I love you," but true love is demonstrated through actions that reflect Christ's heart. Jesus showed His love through healing, serving, and ultimately laying down His life for us.

In your life, there are countless opportunities to show love in action. Whether it's helping a friend in need, volunteering, or simply being present for someone going through a tough time, your actions can speak volumes about God's love.

- Perform a random act of kindness today for someone, whether it's a family member, friend, or stranger. Let your actions reflect God's love in a practical way.

Prayer

Lord, thank You for demonstrating Your love through action. Teach me to love others not just with words, but with deeds that glorify You. Amen.

February 4

Forgiving as Christ Forgives

"Be kind and compassionate to one another, forgiving each other, just as in Christ God forgave you."
Ephesians 4:32

Forgiveness is at the core of Christ's love. Through His sacrifice on the cross, He extended forgiveness to all who believe in Him, regardless of their past. Similarly, we are called to forgive others, not because they deserve it, but because we've been forgiven ourselves.

Holding onto bitterness or resentment can weigh down our hearts and hinder our ability to love freely. Forgiving someone isn't always easy, but it's a choice that leads to healing and restoration. When we forgive, we mirror God's grace and open the door for His love to flow through us.

Think about a situation where forgiveness is needed in your life. How can you take the first step toward reconciliation?

- Reflect on someone you need to forgive. Pray for strength and grace to let go of resentment and extend forgiveness. If possible, reach out to them in kindness, offering words of reconciliation.

Prayer

Lord, thank You for forgiving me completely and unconditionally. Help me to forgive others as You have forgiven me. Teach me to release bitterness and replace it with compassion and grace. Amen.

February 5

Loving Through Service

"Carry each other's burdens, and in this way you will fulfill the law of Christ."
Galatians 6:2

One of the most powerful ways to love others is by serving them. Jesus modeled this perfectly when He washed His disciples' feet, an act of humility and love. Serving others requires us to look beyond our own needs and focus on the well-being of those around us.

When we carry each other's burdens, we reflect the heart of Christ. This might mean offering emotional support, helping with practical needs, or simply being present for someone during a difficult time. Love expressed through service builds deeper connections and glorifies God.

How can you serve someone today in a way that demonstrates Christ's love?

- Find a way to serve someone in your community, church, or family this week. Offer your time, skills, or resources to meet a specific need. Let your actions reflect the love of Christ.

Prayer

Lord, thank You for showing me how to love through service. Open my eyes to the needs around me and give me a willing heart to serve others with humility and joy. Amen.

February 6

Patience in Love

"Love is patient, love is kind. It does not envy, it does not boast, it is not proud."
1 Corinthians 13:4

Patience is a vital part of loving others. It means enduring difficult moments, extending grace when others fall short, and waiting with kindness when things don't go as planned. God shows us perfect patience, allowing us time to grow and transform through His love.

Loving with patience can be challenging, especially when dealing with frustrating situations or people. However, patience reflects Christ's character and strengthens relationships. When you choose patience over irritation, you demonstrate a love that is steadfast and enduring.

Ask yourself: Are there moments where impatience hinders your ability to love well? How can you practice patience today?

- When faced with a challenging situation or person today, pause and pray for patience. Choose to respond with grace and kindness, even if it requires personal sacrifice.

Prayer

Lord, Your love for me is so patient and enduring. Help me to reflect that same patience in my relationships. Teach me to respond with grace, even when it's difficult. Thank You for Your unwavering love. Amen.

February 7

Perfect Love Casts Out Fear

"There is no fear in love. But perfect love drives out fear, because fear has to do with punishment. The one who fears is not made perfect in love."

1 John 4:18

God's perfect love brings peace and security, removing fear and uncertainty. When we experience His love, we can share it with others without fear of rejection or failure. Loving others doesn't mean we'll always be loved in return, but God's love empowers us to give freely, knowing our worth is found in Him.

Perfect love casts out fear by reminding us that God is in control. When we rest in His love, we no longer need to fear vulnerability, judgment, or the future. Instead, we can confidently love others, knowing that His perfect love sustains us.

Consider: Are there fears or insecurities holding you back from loving others fully? Trust God's love to give you courage.

- Reflect on an area of your life where fear has hindered your ability to love freely. Surrender that fear to God and step out in faith by showing love in that area.

Prayer

Lord, thank You for Your perfect love that casts out all fear. Help me to rest in Your love and to love others without hesitation or fear. Teach me to trust in Your unfailing love. Amen.

6

Forgiveness in Difficult Relationships

February 8

The Call to Forgive

"Then Peter came to Jesus and asked, 'Lord, how many times shall I forgive my brother or sister who sins against me? Up to seven times?' Jesus answered, 'I tell you, not seven times, but seventy-seven times.'"
Matthew 18:21-22

Forgiveness is one of the most challenging aspects of our faith. When Peter asked Jesus how often he should forgive, he likely thought he was being generous. Jesus' response—seventy-seven times—wasn't about keeping count but about living in a posture of continual forgiveness.

Forgiveness doesn't mean excusing wrong behavior or pretending the hurt didn't happen. Instead, it's a decision to release the offense and trust God with the outcome. Holding onto bitterness and resentment can poison your heart and block your spiritual growth. When you forgive, you not only obey Christ's command but also free yourself from the burden of anger and pain.

Think about someone who has hurt you deeply. Forgiveness might seem impossible, but Jesus calls us to lean on His strength to forgive, just as He has forgiven us.

- Take time to reflect on any grudges or resentment you may be holding onto. Write down the names of people you need to forgive and pray for each one, asking God to help you release the hurt.

Prayer

Lord, thank You for forgiving me completely and unconditionally. Teach me to forgive others with the same grace. Help me to release bitterness and trust You to heal my heart. Amen.

February 9

The Weight of Unforgiveness

"Get rid of all bitterness, rage and anger, brawling and slander, along with every form of malice. Be kind and compassionate to one another, forgiving each other, just as in Christ God forgave you."
Ephesians 4:31-32

Unforgiveness can feel like a protective shield, but in reality, it's a heavy burden that weighs down your spirit. Bitterness, anger, and resentment only serve to deepen the wounds caused by difficult relationships. Paul's words in Ephesians remind us to let go of these destructive emotions and replace them with kindness and compassion.

Imagine carrying a heavy backpack everywhere you go. The longer you carry it, the more exhausting it becomes. Unforgiveness is like that backpack—it drains your emotional and spiritual energy. Letting go doesn't excuse the other person's actions; it's about freeing yourself from the grip of bitterness and allowing God to bring healing.

Reflect on areas in your life where unforgiveness has taken root. Ask God to help you release these burdens and embrace His peace.

- Identify one area where bitterness has taken hold. Choose one small step toward forgiveness today, such as praying for the person who hurt you or seeking wise counsel to process your emotions.

Prayer

Lord, I confess the weight of unforgiveness in my heart. Help me to release bitterness and anger and to replace them with Your peace and compassion. Thank You for Your grace. Amen.

February 10

Forgiveness Is a Choice

"Bear with each other and forgive one another if any of you has a grievance against someone. Forgive as the Lord forgave you."

Colossians 3:13

Forgiveness begins with a choice, not a feeling. It's a deliberate decision to obey God's command and to release the offense. Feelings of hurt and anger may linger, but forgiveness is the first step toward healing and restoration.

The choice to forgive reflects our understanding of God's forgiveness toward us. We didn't earn or deserve His grace, yet He freely gave it. When we choose to forgive, we mirror His love and extend His grace to others.

This doesn't mean forgiveness is easy. It often requires daily surrender and reliance on God's strength. But each time you choose forgiveness, you take a step closer to the freedom and peace that God desires for you.

- Ask God to reveal any areas in your heart where you need to choose forgiveness. Take a step today by declaring your decision to forgive in prayer, even if the feelings haven't caught up yet.

Prayer

Lord, thank You for forgiving me completely. I choose to forgive those who have hurt me, trusting You to heal my heart and bring restoration. Strengthen me to walk in forgiveness daily. Amen.

February 11

Forgiveness and Reconciliation

"If it is possible, as far as it depends on you, live at peace with everyone."
Romans 12:18

Forgiveness and reconciliation are often misunderstood as the same thing. While forgiveness is a personal decision to release someone from their offense, reconciliation requires mutual effort and trust to rebuild the relationship. Forgiveness is always possible, but reconciliation may not always occur, especially if the other person is unwilling or unsafe.

Paul's words remind us to do everything we can to live at peace with others, but he acknowledges that it's not always fully in our control. The goal of forgiveness is to free your heart from bitterness, whether or not reconciliation happens. If God opens the door to reconciliation, it should be approached with wisdom, prayer, and boundaries as needed.

Ask yourself: Are there relationships where God may be calling you to pursue peace? Or are there situations where forgiveness is enough, even without full reconciliation?

- Reflect on a broken relationship in your life. Pray about whether reconciliation is possible. If so, take a small step, such as reaching out with kindness. If not, commit to forgiving and entrusting the relationship to God.

Prayer

Lord, help me to pursue peace as far as it depends on me. Give me wisdom to know when to seek reconciliation and courage to forgive even when reconciliation isn't possible. Thank You for being my ultimate source of peace. Amen.

February 12

The Healing Power of Forgiveness

"But if you do not forgive others their sins, your Father will not forgive your sins."
Matthew 6:15

Forgiveness is not only about freeing the other person—it's also about freeing yourself. When we refuse to forgive, we create a barrier between ourselves and God. Jesus emphasizes the importance of forgiveness in the Lord's Prayer, reminding us that it's a reflection of our relationship with Him.

Unforgiveness can manifest in bitterness, stress, or even physical symptoms. Forgiveness, on the other hand, brings healing. It allows God's love to flow freely in our lives, mending our hearts and restoring our peace.

Consider the areas in your life where unforgiveness may be holding you back. Are you willing to release the hurt and trust God for healing?

- Spend time in prayer, asking God to help you release any lingering resentment. Write a letter (even if you don't send it) to someone who has hurt you, expressing your forgiveness as a way to unburden your heart.

Prayer

Lord, I want to experience the healing that comes through forgiveness. Help me to let go of resentment and to walk in the freedom of Your grace. Heal my heart and restore my peace. Amen.

February 13

Forgiving Yourself

"Therefore, there is now no condemnation for those who are in Christ Jesus."
Romans 8:1

Sometimes, the hardest person to forgive is yourself. Past mistakes, failures, or sins can weigh heavily on your heart, even after you've sought God's forgiveness. Yet, God's Word reminds us that there is no condemnation for those who are in Christ. Once you've confessed and repented, God forgives completely and remembers your sins no more (Hebrews 8:12).

Holding onto guilt and shame undermines the power of Christ's sacrifice.

Forgiving yourself is an act of faith—it's believing that God's grace is sufficient and that you are no longer defined by your past.

Ask yourself: Are there areas where you're holding onto guilt or shame? Trust in God's promise of forgiveness and allow yourself to move forward in freedom.

- Write down any past mistakes you struggle to forgive yourself for. Bring them to God in prayer, thanking Him for His forgiveness. Then, tear up the paper as a symbolic act of releasing your guilt.

Prayer

Lord, thank You for Your complete forgiveness. Help me to see myself through Your eyes and to release the guilt and shame I've been carrying. Teach me to walk in the freedom of Your grace. Amen.

February 14

Forgiving as Christ Forgives

"Father, forgive them, for they do not know what they are doing."
Luke 23:34

Jesus' words on the cross are the ultimate example of forgiveness. In the midst of His suffering, He forgave those who were responsible for His pain. This powerful act of grace reminds us that forgiveness is not based on the offender's repentance but on our decision to follow Christ's example.

Forgiving as Christ forgives requires a heart transformed by His love. It means surrendering your right to revenge or retribution and trusting God to handle justice. When you forgive, you demonstrate the same mercy that was extended to you through Jesus.

Reflect on how Christ's forgiveness has changed your life. How can you extend that same grace to others, even in the face of deep hurt?

- Meditate on Jesus' forgiveness for you and ask Him to give you the strength to forgive others in the same way. Write down a prayer of forgiveness for someone who has deeply hurt you, and surrender the situation to God.

Prayer

Lord, Your forgiveness is my example and my strength. Help me to forgive as You have forgiven me, even when it feels impossible. Teach me to surrender my hurt to You and to trust in Your perfect justice. Amen.

7

God's Love in Singleness and Marriage

February 15

God's Love is Unchanging

"Give thanks to the Lord, for He is good; His love endures forever."

Psalm 107:1

God's love is a constant in every season of life, whether you're single or married. Human relationships, as fulfilling as they can be, are not designed to replace the perfect love of God. While marriage may offer companionship, and singleness may bring unique opportunities, neither defines your worth. God's love remains unchanging, offering security and purpose regardless of your relationship status.

It's easy to fall into the trap of believing that happiness or completeness depends on another person. Yet, God's love fills every void and sustains us in every circumstance. In singleness, His love provides companionship and purpose. In marriage, His love becomes the foundation for unity and grace.

No matter your current season, God's love is sufficient. Reflect on the truth that His love is unconditional and eternal—it never fluctuates based on your circumstances.

- Spend time reflecting on God's love for you. Write down ways you've

47

experienced His faithfulness in both joyful and challenging seasons. Thank Him for His unchanging love.

Prayer

Lord, thank You for Your steadfast love that never changes. Help me to rest in Your love and find my identity and purpose in You, regardless of my relationship status. Amen.

February 16

Finding Fulfillment in Christ

"For *He satisfies the longing soul, and the hungry soul He fills with good things.*"
Psalm 107:9

In a world that often equates fulfillment with romantic relationships, it's easy to feel incomplete if you're single or to expect your spouse to meet every emotional need if you're married. Yet, true fulfillment comes from Christ alone. He is the only one who can satisfy the deepest longings of your heart.

Singleness offers a unique opportunity to focus on building a deeper relationship with Christ without the responsibilities of marriage. Similarly, marriage is an opportunity to reflect Christ's love through the covenant relationship with your spouse. In both seasons, God calls us to seek Him first and find our fulfillment in Him.

Instead of looking to people or circumstances to complete you, trust God to be your source of joy and contentment. He is enough, and He longs to fill your life with His goodness.

- Examine your heart: Are there areas where you're seeking fulfillment outside of Christ? Spend time in prayer and Bible study, asking God to fill those spaces with His presence.

Prayer

Lord, You are my ultimate source of joy and fulfillment. Help me to seek You above all else and to trust You to satisfy the longings of my heart. Thank You for Your abundance and grace. Amen.

February 17

Singleness as a Season of Purpose

"I would like you to be free from concern. An unmarried man is concerned about the Lord's affairs—how he can please the Lord."

1 Corinthians 7:32

Singleness is often seen as a waiting period, but it's much more than that. Paul reminds us in 1 Corinthians 7 that singleness offers a unique freedom to focus on serving the Lord without the distractions of marital responsibilities. It's a season filled with purpose, not just preparation.

Rather than viewing singleness as a time of lack, embrace it as an opportunity to grow in your relationship with God, pursue your calling, and serve others. God has a purpose for every season, and singleness is no exception. By dedicating this time to Him, you can experience a deeper sense of joy and fulfillment.

If you're single, consider how you can use this season to glorify God. If you're married, encourage those in your life who are single to see their value and purpose in Christ.

- List ways you can use your current season of life to serve God and others. Commit to one specific action this week, such as volunteering, mentoring, or starting a new project.

Prayer

Lord, thank You for the gift of this season. Help me to see its purpose and to use my time and energy to serve You. Teach me to trust Your timing and to embrace Your plans for my life. Amen.

February 18
Marriage as a Reflection of Christ's Love

"Husbands, love your wives, just as Christ loved the church and gave Himself up
for her."
Ephesians 5:25

Marriage is a sacred covenant that reflects the relationship between Christ and His church. In Ephesians, Paul describes the sacrificial love Christ has for His bride, the church. This love is the model for how spouses are to love and serve one another.

Marriage is not just about companionship or happiness; it's about demonstrating God's love and grace. It requires humility, selflessness, and a commitment to put the other person's needs above your own. When a husband and wife love each other as Christ loves the church, their marriage becomes a powerful testimony of God's love to the world.

If you're married, ask yourself: How can I better reflect Christ's love in my relationship? If you're single, consider how you can prepare your heart for a Christ-centered relationship in the future.

- If you're married, commit to one intentional act of love or service for your spouse today. If you're single, pray for wisdom and guidance in preparing your heart for a God-honoring relationship.

Prayer

Lord, thank You for the gift of marriage as a reflection of Your love. Teach me to love selflessly and to honor You in my relationships. Help me to grow in grace and humility. Amen.

February 19

Trusting God's Timing

"He has made everything beautiful in its time. He has also set eternity in the
human heart; yet no one can fathom what God has done from beginning to end."

Ecclesiastes 3:11

In a world that often pressures us to meet certain milestones by specific ages—marriage, children, or career success—it's easy to feel like you're falling behind. Whether single or married, it's crucial to trust in God's perfect timing. His plans for your life are far greater than anything you could imagine.

God's timing isn't always easy to understand, but it's always purposeful. Delays or unanswered prayers may seem discouraging, but they are often God's way of protecting or preparing you for something better. In the waiting, God shapes your character, deepens your faith, and reminds you that His love and sovereignty are sufficient.

Instead of comparing your journey to others, focus on what God is doing in your life right now. Trust that He is making everything beautiful in its time, whether you're waiting for marriage, navigating singleness, or seeking growth within your marriage.

- Surrender your timeline to God. Write down the areas where you feel impatient or discouraged and pray over them, asking God to help you trust His timing.

Prayer

Lord, Your timing is perfect, even when I don't understand it. Help me to trust in Your plans and to find peace in Your love, knowing that You are making everything beautiful in its time. Amen.

February 20
The Gift of Contentment
"I have learned to be content whatever the circumstances."
Philippians 4:11

Contentment is a gift that allows us to experience peace and joy regardless of our circumstances. Paul's words in Philippians remind us that contentment isn't tied to external factors like marital status or life achievements—it comes from a heart rooted in Christ.

In singleness, contentment means embracing the freedom to serve God wholeheartedly. In marriage, it means finding joy in the covenant you've made, even during challenging seasons. In both cases, contentment is not passive resignation but an active trust in God's provision and plan.

Discontentment often stems from focusing on what we lack instead of what we have. When you shift your perspective to gratitude for God's blessings, you can find peace in the present moment. Whether single or married, God's love is your ultimate source of contentment.

- Start a gratitude journal. Each day, write down three things you're thankful for, focusing on the blessings in your current season of life.

Prayer

Lord, teach me to be content in every circumstance. Help me to see the blessings You've given me and to trust that You are enough. Thank You for Your faithfulness and love. Amen.

February 21

Living in God's Love

"And so we know and rely on the love God has for us. God is love. Whoever lives in love lives in God, and God in them."

1 John 4:16

At the core of both singleness and marriage is the call to live in God's love. His love is not just something we receive; it's something we're called to embody and share. Whether you're single or married, your life can be a reflection of God's love to the world.

Living in God's love means prioritizing your relationship with Him above all else. It means extending grace, patience, and kindness to those around you, whether that's a spouse, family, friends, or strangers. God's love is transformative, and when you live in it, your life becomes a testimony of His goodness.

As you navigate your journey, remember that your ultimate identity is not found in your marital status but in being a beloved child of God. His love defines you, sustains you, and calls you to a life of purpose and joy.

- Reflect on ways you can live out God's love in your daily interactions. Commit to one act of kindness or encouragement today that reflects His love to others.

Prayer

Lord, thank You for the gift of Your love. Help me to live in it daily and to share it with those around me. Teach me to rely on Your love as the foundation of my life, whether in singleness or marriage. Amen.

8

Restoring Broken Connections

F**ebruary 22**

The Call to Reconciliation

"All this is from God, who reconciled us to Himself through Christ and gave us the ministry of reconciliation."

2 Corinthians 5:18

Reconciliation is at the heart of God's plan for humanity. Through Christ, God reconciled us to Himself, mending the broken relationship caused by sin. Now, as recipients of His grace, we are called to be agents of reconciliation in our relationships.

Broken connections often stem from misunderstandings, pride, or unresolved hurt. Left unaddressed, these fractures can grow, creating barriers between us and others. However, God's Word reminds us that reconciliation isn't just about fixing relationships—it's about reflecting His love and grace.

Reconciliation requires humility and a willingness to forgive, just as God forgave us. It also requires courage to take the first step, even when it feels uncomfortable. As we embrace the ministry of reconciliation, we mirror God's love and invite His healing into our relationships.

- Identify a strained relationship in your life. Pray for guidance and ask God to show you how to take the first step toward reconciliation, whether through a conversation, a letter, or an act of kindness.

Prayer

Lord, thank You for reconciling me to Yourself through Christ. Help me to reflect Your grace by seeking reconciliation in my relationships. Give me the courage and wisdom to take the first step toward restoring broken connections. Amen.

February 23
Healing Through Forgiveness

"Bear with each other and forgive one another if any of you has a grievance against someone. Forgive as the Lord forgave you."
Colossians 3:13

Forgiveness is the foundation of healing broken relationships. Without it, bitterness and resentment can take root, creating emotional and spiritual barriers. When we forgive, we release the burden of anger and open the door to restoration.

God's forgiveness is our ultimate example. Despite our sin, He extends grace and wipes our slate clean. In the same way, we are called to forgive others—not because they deserve it, but because we have been forgiven. Forgiveness is not condoning the wrong; it is releasing the offender and trusting God to bring justice and healing.

Consider the weight of unforgiveness you might be carrying. Letting go doesn't mean forgetting or excusing the hurt, but it does mean choosing freedom over bondage. As you forgive, you make room for God's peace to fill your heart.

- Take a moment to write down the name of someone you need to forgive and why. Pray over it, asking God for the strength to release the hurt and choose forgiveness.

Prayer

Lord, help me to forgive as You have forgiven me. Free my heart from bitterness and fill it with Your peace. Teach me to extend grace, trusting You to heal what is broken. Amen.

February 24
Overcoming Pride in Relationships

"Do nothing out of selfish ambition or vain conceit. Rather, in humility value others above yourselves."
Philippians 2:3

Pride is one of the greatest obstacles to restoring broken connections. It keeps us from admitting our mistakes, apologizing, or even acknowledging the other person's perspective. Yet, humility is the key to healing relationships.

Jesus modeled perfect humility by leaving His heavenly throne to serve and save humanity. His life and sacrifice remind us that true strength is found in putting others first. In our relationships, humility allows us to let go of the need to be right and focus on what truly matters—restoration and love.

If pride has been a barrier in one of your relationships, consider how you can humble yourself. It might mean being the first to apologize, listening more, or seeking to understand the other person's feelings.

- Reflect on your recent interactions. Identify moments where pride may have hindered connection. Commit to approaching those situations with humility and grace moving forward.

Prayer
Lord, forgive me for the times pride has damaged my relationships. Teach

me to walk in humility, valuing others above myself. Help me to seek restoration with a heart that reflects Your love. Amen.

February 25

The Role of Patience in Restoration

"Be completely humble and gentle; be patient, bearing with one another in love."

Ephesians 4:2

Restoring broken connections often takes time. Healing doesn't happen overnight, especially when trust has been broken or deep wounds exist. Patience is essential in the process of reconciliation.

God demonstrates incredible patience with us, giving us time to repent and grow in our faith. In the same way, we are called to bear with one another in love. This means being gentle when emotions are raw, allowing time for the other person to process, and trusting God to work in their heart.

Impatience can lead to frustration and setbacks. But when we approach restoration with a patient spirit, we create an environment where healing can flourish. Trust God's timing and remain steadfast in love.

- Practice patience by giving space and time to a strained relationship in your life. Pray daily for the other person and trust God to work behind the scenes.

Prayer

Lord, thank You for Your patience with me. Help me to extend that same patience to others as I seek to restore broken connections. Teach me to trust Your timing and to love with gentleness and grace. Amen.

February 26

Speaking Truth in Love

"Instead, speaking the truth in love, we will grow to become in every respect the

mature body of Him who is the head, that is, Christ."
Ephesians 4:15

Restoration requires honesty. Avoiding difficult conversations may feel easier, but unresolved issues often lead to deeper fractures. Speaking truth in love is about addressing problems with kindness and respect, aiming for healing rather than blame.

Jesus exemplified this balance perfectly. He spoke truth to those around Him, yet His words were always rooted in love. In the same way, we must approach our conversations with a heart of compassion, seeking to build up rather than tear down.

If you've been avoiding a necessary conversation, pray for the courage to speak truthfully and lovingly. Trust that God will guide your words and bring clarity to the situation.

- Prepare for a difficult conversation by praying beforehand and focusing on your tone and intention. Write down your thoughts to ensure your words are constructive and compassionate.

Prayer

Lord, help me to speak truth in love. Give me the courage to address conflicts with grace and the wisdom to choose words that bring healing and unity. Amen.

February 27

Choosing Peace Over Conflict

"If it is possible, as far as it depends on you, live at peace with everyone."
Romans 12:18

Conflict is a natural part of relationships, but God calls us to be peacemakers. Living at peace doesn't mean avoiding conflict or pretending everything is fine. Instead, it means actively seeking resolution and harmony whenever possible.

Being a peacemaker requires humility, grace, and intentionality. It often involves laying down your own pride or hurt for the sake of reconciliation. Peace is not about winning an argument but about restoring a connection.

God's peace is our example. Even when humanity rebelled against Him, He made the first move toward reconciliation through Jesus Christ. In the same way, we are called to take steps toward peace in our relationships, relying on God's wisdom and love to guide us.

If a relationship in your life is strained, consider how you can be a peacemaker. It might mean apologizing, letting go of grudges, or initiating a conversation. Trust that God will bless your efforts to live at peace with others.

- Identify an area of conflict in one of your relationships. Pray for God's wisdom and take a step toward peace, whether through a heartfelt apology, a kind gesture, or simply offering forgiveness in your heart.

Prayer

Lord, thank You for the peace You offer through Christ. Help me to be a peacemaker in my relationships, seeking resolution and harmony. Give me the strength and wisdom to choose peace over conflict. Amen.

February 28

Restoring Through Love

"Above all, love each other deeply, because love covers over a multitude of sins."
1 Peter 4:8

At the core of every restored relationship is love. Love is the most powerful force for healing and reconciliation. It softens hardened hearts, mends wounds, and bridges divides.

Peter reminds us that love covers a multitude of sins. This doesn't mean that love ignores wrongs, but that it forgives, endures, and works toward restoration. Love prioritizes the relationship over the hurt, choosing to see the other person through the lens of God's grace.

God's love for us is the ultimate example of restorative love. Despite our flaws and failures, He loves us unconditionally and continuously seeks relationship with us. When we allow His love to flow through us, it empowers us to extend the same grace and compassion to others.

No matter how broken a connection may seem, love can pave the way to healing. By choosing love, you reflect God's heart and open the door to restoration.

- Think of someone with whom you have a strained or distant relationship. Commit to one intentional act of love this week—whether it's a kind word, a thoughtful note, or simply praying for them.

Prayer

Lord, thank You for Your unfailing love that restores and heals. Help me to love others deeply, even when it's difficult. Use Your love through me to mend broken connections and bring peace. Amen.

III

March: Strength in Challenges

9

Finding Peace in Chaos

M**arch 1**

God's Promise of Peace

"Peace I leave with you; my peace I give you. I do not give to you as the world gives. Do not let your hearts be troubled and do not be afraid."

John 14:27

In times of chaos, it's easy to feel overwhelmed and anxious. Life's uncertainties—whether they stem from personal struggles, global events, or day-to-day challenges—can leave us searching for peace. But Jesus offers a peace that transcends circumstances, a peace unlike anything the world can provide.

Jesus spoke these words to His disciples as He prepared for the cross, knowing they would soon face fear and confusion. Yet, He assured them of His peace—a deep, abiding calm that comes from trusting in Him. This peace is not the absence of trouble but the presence of Christ in the midst of it.

When chaos threatens to steal your joy, remember that God's peace is available to you. It's a gift, not something you have to earn. By turning to Him in prayer, meditating on His Word, and trusting His promises, you can experience a calm that anchors your soul.

- When you feel overwhelmed, pause and take a deep breath. Say a short prayer, asking God to fill you with His peace. Write down one promise from Scripture that reminds you of God's faithfulness and keep it where you can see it throughout the day.

Prayer

Lord, thank You for the gift of Your peace. In the midst of chaos, help me to trust in Your presence and promises. Guard my heart and mind with Your peace that surpasses all understanding. Amen.

March 2

Casting Your Cares on God

"Cast all your anxiety on Him because He cares for you."
1 Peter 5:7

Anxiety often builds when we try to carry burdens that were never meant for us to bear. We attempt to solve every problem, control every outcome, and anticipate every challenge, leaving us exhausted and overwhelmed. But God invites us to cast our cares on Him, trusting that He is big enough to handle them and loving enough to want to.

To cast your cares on God means to release them to Him fully. It's an act of surrender, acknowledging that He is sovereign and you are not. This doesn't mean you ignore your responsibilities, but that you entrust the outcome to Him.

God's care is personal and intentional. He knows your struggles and longs to give you peace in exchange for your worries. When you bring your burdens to Him in prayer, you are reminded that you are not alone, and that His strength is sufficient for whatever you face.

- Take a piece of paper and write down everything that is causing you anxiety. Pray over each item, asking God to take control of it. Then tear up or throw away the paper as a physical act of releasing your burdens to Him.

Prayer

Father, thank You for caring for me so deeply. I give You my worries, fears, and anxieties, trusting that You will handle them. Help me to rest in Your love and provision, knowing You are always in control. Amen.

March 3

Guarding Your Heart and Mind

"And the peace of God, which transcends all understanding, will guard your hearts and your minds in Christ Jesus."

Philippians 4:7

When life feels chaotic, our thoughts can spiral into fear, worry, and doubt. But God's peace acts as a shield, guarding our hearts and minds against the attacks of anxiety and despair. This peace is not something we manufacture; it comes as a result of surrendering our thoughts and emotions to Christ.

Paul wrote these words to the Philippians while he was imprisoned—a situation filled with uncertainty and hardship. Yet, he experienced God's peace because he chose to focus on prayer and thanksgiving rather than his circumstances.

God's peace doesn't mean your problems will instantly disappear. Instead, it offers a supernatural calm that allows you to navigate life's challenges with confidence in His presence and promises. By dwelling on His truth and surrendering your worries to Him, you can protect your heart and mind from chaos.

- Whenever you feel anxious, pause and pray. Replace worrisome thoughts with Scripture. Memorize Philippians 4:6-7 and repeat it whenever you need to refocus your mind on God's peace.

Prayer

Lord, thank You for the peace that guards my heart and mind. Teach me to focus on You rather than my circumstances. Help me to rest in Your promises and trust in Your goodness. Amen.

March 4

Trusting God's Plan

"For I know the plans I have for you," declares the Lord, "plans to prosper you and not to harm you, plans to give you hope and a future."
Jeremiah 29:11

When chaos disrupts your life, it's natural to question God's plan. The unexpected twists and turns can leave you feeling lost or confused. However, Jeremiah 29:11 reminds us that God's plans are always good, even when they don't make sense in the moment.

The Israelites received this promise during their exile in Babylon, a time of uncertainty and despair. Though they longed for immediate deliverance, God assured them that He was working for their ultimate good, even in the midst of hardship. Similarly, you can trust that God's plans for you are filled with hope and purpose, even when life feels chaotic.

Trusting God's plan requires surrender and faith. It means believing that His wisdom is greater than yours and that He is working all things together for your good (Romans 8:28). As you trust Him, you will find peace, knowing that He is in control, even in the most challenging circumstances.

- Reflect on a situation in your life that feels chaotic or uncertain. Write a prayer surrendering that situation to God and ask Him to help you trust His plan. Keep this prayer in a journal and revisit it as you see His faithfulness unfold.

Prayer

Lord, thank You for having a good and perfect plan for my life. When chaos surrounds me, help me to trust in Your wisdom and timing.

Strengthen my faith and remind me that You are always working for my good. Amen.

March 5

The Power of Gratitude in Chaos

"Give thanks in all circumstances; for this is God's will for you in Christ Jesus."
1 Thessalonians 5:18

Gratitude might seem impossible when life feels chaotic, but it is one of the most powerful tools for finding peace. When you choose to thank God, even in difficult circumstances, you shift your focus from what's wrong to His faithfulness and provision.

Paul's instruction to give thanks in all circumstances doesn't mean ignoring pain or pretending everything is fine. Instead, it's about acknowledging that God is present and at work, even in the mess. Gratitude transforms your perspective, reminding you of His goodness and giving you hope for the future.

When life feels overwhelming, take time to count your blessings. You'll find that even in the midst of chaos, there is much to be thankful for. Gratitude not only brings peace to your heart but also strengthens your faith in God's unwavering care.

- Create a gratitude journal. Each day, write down three things you're thankful for, no matter how small. Use this practice to shift your focus from worry to worship.

Prayer

Lord, thank You for Your constant presence and provision. Help me to cultivate a heart of gratitude, even in difficult times. Remind me of Your faithfulness and fill my heart with peace as I trust in You. Amen.

March 6

Resting in God's Presence

"Be still, and know that I am God."
Psalm 46:10

In a world that constantly demands action, rest can feel like a luxury. However, God invites you to be still and rest in His presence, especially when life feels chaotic. This stillness isn't about doing nothing; it's about trusting Him and allowing His peace to calm your spirit.

The psalmist's call to "be still" is a reminder that God is sovereign over every situation. When you pause to acknowledge His power and presence, you're reminded that you don't have to carry your burdens alone. Resting in God doesn't mean all your problems will disappear, but it does mean you'll find the strength and peace to face them.

Take time each day to sit quietly with God. Turn off distractions and let His Word and Spirit refresh your soul. In the stillness, you'll discover that His peace is deeper than any chaos you're facing.

- Set aside 10–15 minutes of quiet time each day to be still before God. Read a favorite Scripture, pray, and simply rest in His presence without distractions.

Prayer

Lord, in the midst of life's chaos, teach me to be still and rest in Your presence. Help me to trust in Your power and provision, finding peace in the knowledge that You are always in control. Amen.

March 7

Living as a Peacemaker

"Blessed are the peacemakers, for they will be called children of God."
Matthew 5:9

Finding peace in chaos isn't just about receiving peace for yourself—it's also about sharing that peace with others. Jesus calls us to be peacemakers, bringing His light and love to a world filled with conflict and confusion.

Being a peacemaker requires courage, humility, and a deep trust in God. It means seeking reconciliation in broken relationships, speaking words of kindness, and creating harmony wherever you go. As you live out this calling, you reflect God's character and demonstrate His love to those around you.

Living as a peacemaker doesn't mean avoiding conflict or pretending everything is fine. Instead, it means pursuing truth and love in every situation. As you share God's peace with others, you'll find that His peace grows even stronger in your own heart.

- Look for ways to bring peace to your relationships and community this week. It might mean resolving a conflict, encouraging someone who is struggling, or praying for unity in your church or workplace.

Prayer

Lord, thank You for the peace You have given me. Help me to be a peacemaker, sharing Your love and light in a world filled with chaos. Use me to bring reconciliation and harmony, reflecting Your heart to those around me. Amen.

10

God's Strength in Weakness

March 8

His Grace is Sufficient

"But he said to me, 'My grace is sufficient for you, for my power is made perfect in weakness.' Therefore I will boast all the more gladly about my weaknesses, so that Christ's power may rest on me."
2 Corinthians 12:9

Weakness is not something we like to admit. Society values strength, self-sufficiency, and independence, but God's kingdom operates differently. In 2 Corinthians, Paul shares how he pleaded with God to remove his thorn in the flesh. Instead of removing it, God revealed a profound truth: His grace is sufficient, and His power is made perfect in weakness.

Weakness becomes an opportunity for God to show His strength. When you acknowledge your limitations and surrender them to Him, He steps in with His power and grace. Instead of striving to overcome in your own strength, lean into God's sufficiency.

In moments of weakness, remind yourself that it's not about what you can do but what God can do through you. His grace is always enough, and His strength will carry you through any challenge.

Identify an area of weakness in your life. Instead of striving to fix it on

70

your own, surrender it to God in prayer. Ask Him to show His strength in that area and trust in His sufficiency.

Prayer

Lord, thank You for reminding me that Your grace is sufficient for every need. In my weakness, help me to rely on Your strength. May Your power be made perfect in me as I surrender my struggles to You. Amen.

March 9

The Source of True Strength

"I can do all things through Christ who strengthens me."
Philippians 4:13

This verse is often quoted as a source of encouragement, but its true meaning goes beyond achieving personal goals. Paul wrote these words from prison, where he experienced hardship and suffering. His strength came not from his own abilities but from Christ, who empowered him to endure and remain faithful.

God's strength is not about making life easy but about equipping you to persevere through challenges. When you depend on Him, you can face trials, resist temptation, and fulfill your calling with courage and resilience.

Remember, the strength you need doesn't come from within—it comes from your relationship with Christ. By staying connected to Him through prayer, worship, and His Word, you'll find the power to overcome even the toughest circumstances.

- Reflect on an area where you feel weak or inadequate. Write Philippians 4:13 on a card and keep it with you as a reminder to rely on Christ's strength, not your own.

Prayer

Jesus, thank You for being the source of my strength. Teach me to rely on You in every situation, knowing that Your power is sufficient to carry me through. Help me to trust in Your provision and not my own abilities. Amen.

March 10

God's Strength in the Storm

"God is our refuge and strength, an ever-present help in trouble."
Psalm 46:1

Life's storms can leave you feeling battered and overwhelmed, but God promises to be your refuge and strength. He is not distant or detached from your struggles; He is ever-present, ready to provide comfort and power in times of trouble.

When you face difficulties, it's easy to focus on the waves crashing around you. But like Peter walking on water, fixing your eyes on Jesus will keep you steady. God's strength is a safe harbor where you can find peace and rest, even in the midst of chaos.

Trusting God as your refuge doesn't mean the storm will immediately end, but it does mean you won't face it alone. His strength will sustain you, and His presence will give you courage to keep moving forward.

- The next time you feel overwhelmed, take a moment to pause and pray. Visualize God as your refuge—a place of safety and peace. Meditate on Psalm 46:1 and ask Him to be your strength in the storm.

Prayer

Father, thank You for being my refuge and strength. When life feels overwhelming, help me to find peace in Your presence. Remind me that You are with me in every storm, and Your power will sustain me. Amen.

March 11

When You Feel Like Giving Up

"The Lord is my strength and my shield; my heart trusts in him, and he helps me."

Psalm 28:7

There are moments when you feel like giving up, when the weight of life's challenges becomes too heavy to bear. But in those moments, God's strength is your shield, protecting you and lifting you up.

Trusting in God doesn't mean you won't face hardship, but it does mean you won't face it alone. He sees your struggles and offers His help. As you lean on Him, He will renew your strength and give you the courage to keep going.

When you feel weak, remember that God is your strength. He will carry you when you can't carry yourself. Trust in His faithfulness and let Him guide you through the challenges you face.

- Think about an area of your life where you feel like giving up. Spend time in prayer, asking God for renewed strength and courage. Reach out to a trusted friend or mentor for encouragement and support.

Prayer

Lord, when I feel weak and weary, remind me that You are my strength and shield. Help me to trust in Your help and to find courage in Your promises. Thank You for carrying me when I can't carry myself. Amen.

March 12

Strength for the Battle

"The Lord is my light and my salvation—whom shall I fear? The Lord is the stronghold of my life—of whom shall I be afraid?"

Psalm 27:1

Life often feels like a battle, with challenges, doubts, and fears coming at us from every direction. In these moments, it's comforting to remember that God is your strength and protector. He is your stronghold—a place of safety and power where you can find refuge.

David, who wrote this psalm, faced countless battles, both physical and spiritual. Yet, his confidence wasn't in his own ability but in the Lord's power. When you feel overwhelmed by life's battles, remember that you're not fighting alone. God is with you, equipping you with His strength and guiding you through every challenge.

Fear loses its grip when you rely on God's strength. Instead of focusing on what's against you, focus on the One who is for you. He is your light in the darkness, your salvation in trouble, and your unshakable fortress in every storm.

Prayer

Lord, thank You for being my stronghold and my salvation. When I feel afraid or overwhelmed, help me to lean on Your strength and trust in Your protection. Remind me that You are with me in every battle and that Your power is greater than anything I face. Amen.

March 13

Strength Made Perfect in Weakness

"He gives strength to the weary and increases the power of the weak."
Isaiah 40:29

We often view weakness as a flaw, but God sees it as an opportunity to display His power. When you are weary, depleted, or at the end of your rope, God steps in to renew your strength. He doesn't abandon you in your weakness; instead, He meets you there and provides exactly what you need.

Isaiah reminds us that God's strength is limitless. While human effort can only go so far, God's power is infinite. When you feel like you can't go on, remember that God is the One who sustains you. He will lift you up, renew your energy, and give you the strength to keep moving forward.

Instead of hiding your weakness, bring it to God. Acknowledge your need for His help and watch as He transforms your weariness into strength. His grace is more than enough to carry you through.

- Make a list of areas where you feel weak or weary. Pray over each one, asking God to renew your strength and fill you with His power. Memorize Isaiah 40:29 to remind yourself of His promise.

Prayer

Lord, thank You for giving strength to the weary and power to the weak. When I feel depleted, remind me to turn to You. Help me to rely on Your strength and not my own, knowing that Your power is made perfect in my weakness. Amen.

March 14

Walking in God's Strength

"Those who hope in the Lord will renew their strength. They will soar on wings like eagles; they will run and not grow weary, they will walk and not be faint."

Isaiah 40:31

Life is a journey, and it often feels long and exhausting. But those who place their hope in the Lord are promised renewed strength. This doesn't mean life will be free of challenges, but it does mean that God will sustain you every step of the way.

Isaiah paints a beautiful picture of soaring like eagles, running without weariness, and walking without fainting. This imagery reminds us that God's strength is available for every phase of life—whether you're soaring in victory, running through challenges, or walking through daily routines.

Placing your hope in the Lord means trusting His timing, His provision, and His faithfulness. As you walk with Him, He will empower you to face each day with courage and endurance.

- Start each day by committing your journey to God. Pray for His strength to sustain you, whether you're facing big challenges or simply navigating your daily responsibilities. Reflect on how He has renewed your strength in the past, and thank Him for His faithfulness.

Prayed

Father, thank You for renewing my strength when I place my hope in You. Help me to trust in Your provision and walk in Your power each day. Teach me to rely on You in every season, knowing that You will sustain me through it all. Amen.

11

Overcoming Anxiety with Faith

March 15

Casting Your Cares on God

"Cast all your anxiety on Him because He cares for you."
1 Peter 5:7

Anxiety often feels like carrying a heavy backpack filled with worries, fears, and uncertainties. The weight can become overwhelming, leaving you exhausted and discouraged. But God invites you to cast all your cares on Him because He deeply cares for you.

This invitation isn't just for minor worries; it's for every burden that weighs you down. When you cast your cares on God, you're releasing control and trusting Him to handle what you cannot. It's a reminder that He is strong enough to carry your burdens and tender enough to care about your struggles.

Faith grows as you surrender your worries to God. Instead of trying to figure everything out on your own, trust that He is working behind the scenes for your good. Let Him carry your burdens, and you'll find peace replacing anxiety.

• Write down your current anxieties and worries. In prayer, name each one and physically imagine handing it over to God. Keep a list of answered prayers as a reminder of His faithfulness.

Prayer

Lord, thank You for caring about every detail of my life. Help me to cast my anxieties on You and trust in Your love and faithfulness. Teach me to rest in Your peace, knowing that You are in control. Amen.

March 16

Seeking God's Peace

"Do not be anxious about anything, but in every situation, by prayer and petition, with thanksgiving, present your requests to God. And the peace of God, which transcends all understanding, will guard your hearts and your minds in Christ Jesus."

Philippians 4:6–7

Anxiety often stems from feeling out of control, but Philippians 4:6–7 offers a solution: prayer. Instead of letting worries spiral, take them to God with a heart of thanksgiving. When you do, His peace will guard your heart and mind, protecting you from fear and doubt.

God's peace is not the absence of problems but a deep assurance that He is in control. It transcends understanding because it doesn't depend on circumstances. It's a gift that calms your heart and reminds you that God is with you in every situation.

Thanksgiving is a key part of this process. Gratitude shifts your focus from what's wrong to what God has already done. As you thank Him for His faithfulness, your faith grows, and anxiety loses its grip.

- The next time you feel anxious, stop and pray. Present your worries to God and thank Him for His past faithfulness. Write down your prayer to help you release your concerns and trust in His peace.

Prayer

Lord, thank You for Your promise of peace. Help me to bring my anxieties to You in prayer, trusting that You will guard my heart and mind. Teach me to live in gratitude and faith, knowing that You are always in control. Amen.

March 17

Trusting God's Timing

"When I am afraid, I put my trust in You."
Psalm 56:3

Anxiety often arises from uncertainty about the future. Waiting for answers, solutions, or changes can leave you feeling restless and afraid. But Psalm 56:3 reminds us that trust is the antidote to fear. When you choose to trust God's timing, anxiety begins to lose its power.

God's timing is perfect, even when it doesn't match your expectations. Trusting Him requires patience and faith, believing that He is working all things together for your good (Romans 8:28). When fear creeps in, remember that God is faithful and His plans are always better than anything you could imagine.

Faith doesn't eliminate waiting, but it changes how you wait. Instead of worrying about what's ahead, trust that God's timing is always right. Rest in His promises and let His peace guard your heart.

- Reflect on a situation where you're struggling to trust God's timing. Write a prayer surrendering the outcome to Him and ask for the faith to wait patiently. Memorize Psalm 56:3 to remind you to trust Him when fear arises.

Prayer

Father, thank You for Your perfect timing. Help me to trust You when I feel anxious about the future. Teach me to wait with faith, knowing that

Your plans are always good. Calm my fears and fill me with Your peace. Amen.

March 18

Fixing Your Eyes on Jesus

"You will keep in perfect peace those whose minds are steadfast, because they trust in You." Isaiah 26:3

Anxiety often shifts your focus to uncertainties, fears, and "what ifs." These distractions pull you away from the steady assurance of God's presence. Isaiah 26:3 reminds us that perfect peace is found when we keep our minds steadfastly fixed on God and trust in Him.

Fixing your eyes on Jesus means anchoring your thoughts to His promises, His power, and His love. Instead of allowing anxiety to take control, you intentionally focus on who God is—your protector, provider, and peace-giver. This steadfast trust transforms anxious thoughts into peaceful assurance.

When Peter walked on water toward Jesus, he stayed above the waves as long as his eyes were on the Lord. But the moment he focused on the storm, he began to sink (Matthew 14:29–30). In the same way, peace comes when your focus remains on Jesus rather than the storms of life.

- When anxious thoughts arise, pause and pray. Meditate on God's promises or read a Scripture that reminds you of His faithfulness. Commit to focusing on His presence throughout the day by practicing gratitude and worship.

Prayer

Lord, thank You for being my source of perfect peace. Teach me to fix my eyes on You when anxiety threatens to overwhelm me. Help me to trust in Your promises and find rest in Your unfailing love. Amen.

March 19

Surrendering Control to God

"Be still, and know that I am God."
Psalm 46:10

One of the root causes of anxiety is the desire for control. When life feels uncertain or chaotic, you may try to hold on tighter, attempting to manage every detail. But Psalm 46:10 invites you to let go and be still, trusting that God is in control.

Surrender doesn't mean giving up; it means placing your trust in God's sovereignty. It's a reminder that He is God, and you are not. He knows the end from the beginning and has a plan for your life that is good and perfect (Jeremiah 29:11).

When you release your need for control, you open the door for God's peace to flood your heart. Being still before Him allows you to experience His presence and hear His voice, reassuring you that He's got everything under control.

- Identify an area where you've been holding on too tightly. Write it down and surrender it to God in prayer. Practice being still before Him each day by spending a few quiet moments meditating on His Word and trusting in His sovereignty.

Prayer

Father, thank You for being in control of every detail of my life. Help me to let go of my need for control and to trust in Your perfect plan. Teach me to be still before You and to rest in the knowledge that You are God. Amen.

March 20

Replacing Fear with Faith

"For God has not given us a spirit of fear, but of power and of love and of a sound mind."

2 Timothy 1:7

Anxiety often comes from a place of fear—fear of failure, fear of the unknown, or fear of loss. But 2 Timothy 1:7 reminds us that fear is not from God. Instead, He gives you a spirit of power, love, and a sound mind.

God equips you with everything you need to face life's challenges. His power strengthens you, His love surrounds you, and His wisdom guides your decisions. When fear tries to take hold, remind yourself that it has no place in your life because God's Spirit is within you.

Choosing faith over fear is a daily decision. It means standing on God's promises, even when circumstances are uncertain. Faith doesn't deny the reality of your struggles, but it declares that God is greater than your fears.

- The next time you feel fear rising, speak 2 Timothy 1:7 aloud and declare God's truth over your situation. Write down a few of His promises to meditate on when anxiety tries to return.

Prayer

Lord, thank You for giving me a spirit of power, love, and a sound mind. When fear arises, help me to stand on Your promises and trust in Your power. Replace my anxiety with faith and fill me with Your peace. Amen.

March 21

Resting in God's Promises

"Come to me, all you who are weary and burdened, and I will give you rest."
Matthew 11:28

Anxiety can leave you feeling weary and burdened, but Jesus offers an invitation to rest. He doesn't expect you to carry your worries alone. Instead, He invites you to come to Him and lay your burdens at His feet.

Resting in God's promises means trusting that He will take care of you. It's an act of faith to release your worries and believe that He is working all things together for your good. As you rest in His presence, He renews your strength and fills you with His peace.

Jesus doesn't promise a life free of trouble, but He does promise to walk with you through every challenge. His rest is not just physical but also emotional and spiritual. It's a deep assurance that He is in control and that you can trust Him completely.

- Set aside time each day to rest in God's presence. Turn off distractions, read His Word, and spend time in prayer. Write down a few of His promises that bring you peace and reflect on them throughout the week.

Prayer

Jesus, thank You for inviting me to rest in Your presence. Teach me to trust in Your promises and to release my burdens to You. Fill me with Your peace and remind me that You are always in control. Amen.

12

Standing Firm During Life's Storms

March 22

Anchored by Hope
"We have this hope as an anchor for the soul, firm and secure."
Hebrews 6:19

Hope is the anchor that keeps you steady during life's storms. Just as a ship's anchor holds it firmly in place amidst rough seas, your hope in God secures your soul when life feels chaotic. This hope isn't wishful thinking—it's a confident assurance in God's promises and His unchanging character.

When the winds of uncertainty blow, it's easy to drift into fear and despair. But hope in God reminds you that He is faithful and that His plans for you are good. He is the same yesterday, today, and forever, and His promises never fail.

Anchoring your soul in hope requires actively placing your trust in God. It means choosing faith over fear and believing that He will see you through every storm.

- Write down three promises from God's Word that give you hope. Keep them in a place where you can read them daily. When challenges arise, remind yourself of these truths and pray for God to anchor your soul in His peace.

Prayer

Father, thank You for being my anchor in life's storms. Help me to place my hope in You and to trust in Your promises. Strengthen my faith and remind me of Your unfailing love, even in the midst of uncertainty. Amen.

March 23

Peace in the Storm

"He got up, rebuked the wind, and said to the waves, 'Quiet! Be still!' Then the wind died down and it was completely calm."

Mark 4:39

When the disciples were caught in a violent storm, they panicked, fearing for their lives. But Jesus, who was with them in the boat, demonstrated His authority by calming the wind and waves with just a word. His presence brought peace, even in the midst of chaos.

Life's storms can feel overwhelming, leaving you anxious and fearful. But like the disciples, you can call out to Jesus, knowing that He is with you and has the power to calm the storm. Even if the circumstances don't change immediately, His presence brings peace to your heart and mind.

Trusting Jesus in the storm doesn't mean ignoring your fears; it means bringing them to Him and resting in His authority. He is the Prince of Peace, and His peace transcends all understanding (Philippians 4:7).

- The next time you feel overwhelmed, pause and pray. Ask Jesus to calm your heart and give you His peace. Meditate on Mark 4:39 and visualize Him speaking peace into your situation.

Prayer

Lord, thank You for being with me in life's storms. When I feel overwhelmed, help me to turn to You and trust in Your power. Speak peace into my heart and remind me that You are in control. Amen.

March 24

Trusting God's Sovereignty

"And we know that in all things God works for the good of those who love Him, who have been called according to His purpose."

Romans 8:28

When life's storms rage, it's easy to question why things happen the way they do. Unanswered prayers, setbacks, or unexpected trials can make you feel as though God is distant or indifferent. However, Romans 8:28 reminds you that God is sovereign, and He is always working for your good, even in the hardest seasons.

Trusting God's sovereignty doesn't mean you'll understand every detail of His plan. Instead, it's about believing that He is in control and that He is weaving every circumstance—both good and bad—into a tapestry of purpose. Storms may test your faith, but they also refine it, shaping you into the person God created you to be.

Instead of focusing on the chaos around you, fix your heart on the truth that God's ways are higher than your ways (Isaiah 55:8–9). He sees the bigger picture and is faithful to carry you through every storm.

- Reflect on a challenging situation you've faced in the past and how God used it for your good. Write down how His sovereignty brought growth or healing. Let this encourage you to trust Him in your current circumstances.

Prayer

Father, thank You for working all things together for my good. Help me to trust Your sovereignty, even when I don't understand what You're doing. Strengthen my faith and remind me that You are always in control. Amen.

March 25

Standing on God's Promises

"The grass withers and the flowers fall, but the word of our God endures forever."
Isaiah 40:8

Life's storms may come and go, but God's Word remains unchanging. His promises are a firm foundation, providing strength and hope when everything around you feels unstable. Isaiah 40:8 reminds you that while the world is ever-changing, God's truth endures forever.

When anxiety or fear threatens to overwhelm you, stand on His promises. Remind yourself that He is your refuge and strength (Psalm 46:1), that He will never leave you nor forsake you (Deuteronomy 31:8), and that His plans for you are good (Jeremiah 29:11). These promises are not just words; they are eternal truths backed by God's faithfulness.

As you meditate on His Word, your faith will grow stronger, enabling you to stand firm in the face of life's challenges. His promises are a shield, protecting your heart and mind from fear and doubt.

- Choose three promises from Scripture that speak to your current struggles. Write them on index cards or save them on your phone. Read and meditate on them daily, allowing God's truth to replace fear with faith.

Prayer

Lord, thank You for Your unchanging promises. Help me to stand firm on Your Word and to trust in Your faithfulness, even when life feels uncertain. Strengthen my heart and fill me with peace as I rest in Your truth. Amen.

March 26

Persevering Through the Storm

"Blessed is the one who perseveres under trial because, having stood the test, that person will receive the crown of life that the Lord has promised to those who love

Him."
James 1:12

Storms test your faith, but they also build your endurance. James 1:12 encourages you to persevere through trials, reminding you that blessings await those who remain steadfast. Perseverance is not about avoiding the storm but enduring it with faith and hope in God.

God uses storms to refine and strengthen you, much like a fire refines gold. Each trial is an opportunity to grow closer to Him, deepen your trust, and develop spiritual maturity. While the process may be painful, the reward is a stronger, more resilient faith.

Remember that God is with you in every trial, equipping you with the strength to endure. Lean on His presence, His promises, and His power as you navigate life's challenges.

- Identify a current trial and ask God to show you how He's using it to grow your faith. Journal about the ways you've seen His strength sustain you in the past. Let these reminders encourage you to keep persevering.

Prayer

Father, thank You for being my strength in trials. Help me to persevere through life's storms and to trust in Your refining work. Strengthen my faith and remind me of the blessings that come from standing firm in You. Amen.

March 27

Rejoicing in Victory

"But thanks be to God! He gives us the victory through our Lord Jesus Christ."
1 Corinthians 15:57

Life's storms may feel overwhelming, but as a believer, you are assured of ultimate victory in Christ. 1 Corinthians 15:57 reminds you that through Jesus, you have already overcome. No matter how fierce the storm, it cannot separate you from His love or defeat the power of His resurrection.

Victory in Christ doesn't always mean an immediate end to your struggles. Sometimes, it's about experiencing His peace and strength in the midst of the storm. Other times, it's about trusting Him for the ultimate resolution, knowing that He will work all things together for your good.

As you face life's challenges, rejoice in the victory that is yours through Jesus. Let His triumph over sin, death, and every obstacle give you hope and courage to stand firm. The storms may come, but in Christ, you are more than a conqueror (Romans 8:37).

- Celebrate the victories God has already given you, big or small. Share your testimony with someone who may be facing their own storm, encouraging them with the hope and peace you've found in Christ.

Prayer

Lord, thank You for the victory I have in You. Help me to stand firm in faith and to trust in Your power, no matter what storms I face. Fill my heart with joy and gratitude as I rest in the assurance of Your love and victory. Amen.

IV

April: Balancing Life's Demands

13

Prioritizing Time with God

April 1

Seeking God First

"But seek first His kingdom and His righteousness, and all these things will be given to you as well."
Matthew 6:33

In the busyness of life, it's easy to let time with God take a back seat. However, Matthew 6:33 reminds us that seeking God first is the key to living a fulfilled and balanced life. When you make God your priority, everything else falls into place according to His will.

Seeking God first doesn't mean neglecting your responsibilities. It means recognizing that your relationship with Him is the foundation for every other aspect of your life. Just as you need physical nourishment, your soul thrives when it is fed by His presence, Word, and guidance.

Imagine starting your day with God instead of rushing into tasks or distractions. It sets the tone for the rest of your day, aligning your heart with His purposes and giving you the peace and strength to face whatever comes your way.

- Set aside the first few moments of your day to pray and read Scripture, even if it's just five minutes. Commit to making this a daily habit, trusting God to honor your desire to put Him first.

Prayer

Lord, help me to seek You first in everything I do. Teach me to prioritize time with You and to trust that You will provide for my needs. Align my heart with Yours and guide me in all areas of my life. Amen.

April 2

Drawing Near to God

"Come near to God, and He will come near to you."
James 4:8

God desires a close relationship with you. James 4:8 offers a beautiful promise: as you draw near to Him, He draws near to you. But cultivating intimacy with God requires intentionality. Just as a relationship with a friend or loved one deepens through time and communication, your relationship with God grows when you prioritize being in His presence.

Drawing near to God means setting aside distractions and making time for prayer, worship, and studying His Word. It's not about perfection or long hours; it's about a heart that longs to be with Him. Even small, consistent moments spent with God can deepen your connection to Him.

As you intentionally draw near to Him, you'll begin to sense His presence in your life more clearly. You'll experience His peace, guidance, and love in ways that strengthen your faith and bring joy to your heart.

- Choose a quiet place where you can meet with God daily. Use this time to pray, read Scripture, or simply sit in His presence. Reflect on how His nearness impacts your day.

Prayer

Lord, thank You for Your promise to draw near when I seek You. Help me to set aside distractions and to spend intentional time with You each day. May Your presence fill my heart and strengthen my faith. Amen.

April 3

Listening to God's Voice

"Be still, and know that I am God."
Psalm 46:10

In a world filled with noise and busyness, it can be challenging to hear God's voice. Yet Psalm 46:10 reminds you of the importance of stillness—pausing to recognize His presence and listen to His guidance.

Listening to God requires more than just speaking in prayer; it involves quieting your mind and heart to hear Him. God often speaks through His Word, the Holy Spirit, or gentle impressions on your heart. When you take the time to listen, He provides wisdom, comfort, and direction for your life.

Stillness is a spiritual discipline that helps you tune out distractions and focus on God. As you practice listening, you'll become more attuned to His voice, enabling you to follow His lead with confidence and peace.

- Dedicate a few minutes of your prayer time to silence. Ask God to speak to your heart and listen without distractions. Journal any thoughts or impressions you sense from Him.

Prayer

Father, teach me to be still and to listen for Your voice. Help me to quiet the noise in my life and to focus on You. Guide me with Your wisdom and fill my heart with Your peace. Amen.

April 4

Making God Your Daily Bread

"Jesus answered, 'It is written: Man shall not live on bread alone, but on every word that comes from the mouth of God.'"

Matthew 4:4

Just as your body requires food to sustain physical life, your soul requires spiritual nourishment to thrive. In Matthew 4:4, Jesus reminds us that God's Word is essential for life. It sustains, strengthens, and equips you for every challenge and opportunity.

When you make God's Word a daily priority, it transforms your perspective and helps you grow in faith. Regularly feeding on Scripture helps you navigate life with wisdom and peace. It becomes a source of comfort in trials, a guide in decision-making, and a reminder of God's love and promises.

Neglecting spiritual nourishment can leave you feeling spiritually weak and vulnerable. By intentionally seeking God through His Word, you build a strong spiritual foundation that keeps you steady in every season.

- Set aside time each day to read and meditate on Scripture. Start with a manageable goal, like one chapter or a few verses, and reflect on how it applies to your life.

Prayer

Lord, thank You for the gift of Your Word, which nourishes my soul and sustains me. Help me to prioritize spending time in Scripture each day and to apply Your truth in my life. Teach me to rely on You as my daily bread. Amen.

April 5

Overcoming Distractions

"Martha, Martha," the Lord answered, "you are worried and upset about many things, but few things are needed—or indeed only one."

Luke 10:41-42

In the story of Mary and Martha, Martha was consumed by busyness and distractions, while Mary chose to sit at Jesus' feet and listen to Him. Jesus gently reminded Martha that Mary had chosen what was better: time with Him.

Life is full of demands—work, responsibilities, and constant notifications—that can pull your attention away from God. While these things may be important, they should never take precedence over your relationship with Him.

Overcoming distractions requires intentionality. Like Mary, you must choose to focus on Jesus, even when the world demands your attention. This choice may involve setting boundaries, simplifying your schedule, or turning off distractions to create space for God. When you prioritize Him, everything else finds its proper place.

- Identify one distraction that often pulls you away from spending time with God. Take a specific step to minimize or remove it, such as turning off your phone during prayer or setting a daily reminder to pause and spend time with Him.

Prayer

Lord, help me to overcome the distractions that pull me away from You. Teach me to prioritize time in Your presence and to trust that everything else will fall into place when I put You first. Amen.

April 6

Finding Rest in God

"Come to me, all you who are weary and burdened, and I will give you rest."
Matthew 11:28

The demands of life can leave you feeling exhausted, overwhelmed, and spiritually drained. Yet Jesus invites you to come to Him and find rest—not just physical rest, but rest for your soul.

Spending time with God renews your strength and refreshes your spirit.

In His presence, you can lay down your burdens and receive His peace. Resting in God doesn't mean neglecting your responsibilities; it means trusting Him to carry your load and provide what you need.

When you make time for rest in God's presence, you're reminded that He is in control. You don't have to do everything on your own. His strength is sufficient, and His grace is enough to sustain you through every challenge.

- Set aside a day or a specific block of time this week to rest in God's presence. Use this time to pray, worship, or simply reflect on His goodness. Allow Him to renew your strength.

Prayer

Father, thank You for offering rest to my weary soul. Help me to find my peace and renewal in You. Teach me to trust in Your strength and to let go of the burdens I try to carry on my own. Amen.

April 7

Living a Life of Devotion

"Love the Lord your God with all your heart and with all your soul and with all your mind."
Matthew 22:37

Living a life of devotion means making God the center of everything you do. It's not just about spending time with Him in prayer and Scripture, but also about honoring Him in your thoughts, actions, and decisions.

When you love God with all your heart, soul, and mind, your priorities naturally align with His will. Devotion becomes less about checking off spiritual tasks and more about cultivating a relationship with Him. It's about inviting Him into every moment of your life—your joys, struggles, and even the mundane routines.

A life of devotion requires consistency and commitment, but the rewards are eternal. As you prioritize time with God and live for His glory, you'll experience His presence and guidance in every aspect of your life.

- Reflect on your daily routine and identify ways to incorporate devotion to God into every aspect of your life. This could mean starting your day with prayer, inviting Him into your work, or ending your day in gratitude.

Prayer

Lord, I want to live a life of devotion to You. Help me to love You with all my heart, soul, and mind and to honor You in everything I do. Teach me to prioritize our relationship above all else. Amen.

14

Grace for the Overwhelmed Woman

A pril 8

Resting in God's Grace

"My grace is sufficient for you, for my power is made perfect in weakness."

2 Corinthians 12:9

Feeling overwhelmed is a common experience in today's busy world. Whether it's balancing family, work, or personal commitments, the pressure to do it all can leave you exhausted and discouraged. But God's grace is sufficient for every season of life, especially the overwhelming ones.

In 2 Corinthians 12:9, God reminds you that His power is made perfect in your weakness. When you feel inadequate, His grace steps in to provide strength. Resting in His grace means acknowledging your limits and trusting Him to fill the gaps.

You don't have to carry life's burdens alone. God invites you to lean on Him, to find rest in His presence, and to let go of the unrealistic expectations you place on yourself. His grace is not just a concept; it is an active, empowering force that sustains you when you feel like giving up.

• Take a moment to identify areas where you feel overwhelmed. Pray and release those burdens to God. Write down how His grace has sustained you in the past, and let it encourage you today.

Prayer

Lord, thank You for Your grace that is sufficient for me. Help me to rest in Your strength and to trust You with the areas where I feel overwhelmed. Remind me that I don't have to do it all on my own. Amen.

April 9

Letting Go of Perfectionism

"Come to me, all you who are weary and burdened, and I will give you rest."
Matthew 11:28

Perfectionism often fuels the feelings of being overwhelmed. The desire to meet every expectation, fulfill every role flawlessly, and never make mistakes can lead to exhaustion. But Jesus invites you to come to Him and find rest, releasing the burden of perfectionism.

God doesn't expect perfection from you; He desires your heart. When you strive to be perfect, you may miss the beauty of His grace, which covers your imperfections and enables you to live in freedom. Jesus reminds you that His yoke is easy, and His burden is light (Matthew 11:30).

Letting go of perfectionism allows you to embrace God's grace and live with joy and peace. It's okay to have limitations; they remind you of your need for Him.

- Identify one area where you've been striving for perfection. Release it to God in prayer, and commit to embracing grace instead. Focus on doing your best and trusting Him with the outcome.

Prayer

Lord, I surrender my need for perfection to You. Teach me to rest in Your grace and to trust that You are enough. Help me to let go of unrealistic expectations and to find joy in Your presence. Amen.

April 10

Prioritizing What Matters

"Teach us to number our days, that we may gain a heart of wisdom."
Psalm 90:12

Overwhelm often comes from trying to do too much at once. Psalm 90:12 reminds us to ask God for wisdom in how we use our time and energy. When you learn to prioritize what truly matters, you can focus on what aligns with God's will and let go of unnecessary burdens.

Not everything on your to-do list is essential. God calls you to live intentionally, making space for Him and for the people and purposes He's placed in your life. It's about finding balance and letting His wisdom guide your choices.

When you feel overwhelmed, pause and ask God to show you what's most important. He will give you clarity and help you let go of what isn't necessary for this season.

- Review your schedule and commitments. Ask God to help you prioritize what matters most. Consider saying "no" to something that doesn't align with His purpose for you right now.

Prayer

Father, teach me to prioritize what matters most. Give me wisdom to use my time and energy in ways that honor You. Help me to let go of what isn't essential and to trust You with the rest. Amen.

April 11

Strength for Today

"The Lord is my strength and my shield; my heart trusts in Him, and He helps me."

Psalm 28:7

When life feels overwhelming, it's easy to feel like you don't have the strength to get through the day. The truth is, you don't have to rely on your own strength—God is your strength. Psalm 28:7 reminds you that when your heart trusts in Him, He provides the help and endurance you need.

God's strength is not just for monumental challenges; it's for the ordinary demands of daily life. Whether it's managing a packed schedule, handling a difficult conversation, or facing an unexpected challenge, His strength is available to you in every moment.

When you lean on God, you're acknowledging your dependence on Him. This dependence is not a weakness but a source of power. His strength allows you to keep going, even when you feel like giving up.

- Start your day by asking God for His strength to face whatever lies ahead. Throughout the day, take moments to pause and pray for His help when you feel overwhelmed.

Prayer

Lord, You are my strength and my shield. Help me to trust in You completely and to rely on Your power in every moment. Thank You for sustaining me when I feel weak and overwhelmed. Amen.

April 12

God's Peace in the Chaos

"And the peace of God, which transcends all understanding, will guard your hearts and your minds in Christ Jesus."

Philippians 4:7

Amid life's chaos, God offers a peace that surpasses all understanding. This peace doesn't come from having everything under control; it comes from trusting that God is in control. Philippians 4:7 assures you that His peace will guard your heart and mind when you surrender your worries to Him.

When you feel overwhelmed, it's tempting to try to fix everything yourself. But peace comes when you choose to trust God instead of relying on your own strength. It's about giving your concerns to Him in prayer and trusting that He is working for your good, even when you can't see it.

God's peace is not dependent on your circumstances. It is a gift that protects your heart and mind, reminding you of His presence and love no matter what you face.

- When anxiety creeps in, take a deep breath and pray, releasing your worries to God. Meditate on Philippians 4:7 and let His peace fill your heart and mind.

Prayer

Father, thank You for the gift of Your peace that surpasses all understanding. Help me to surrender my worries to You and to trust that You are in control. Guard my heart and mind with Your perfect peace. Amen.

April 13

Grace to Say No

"Let what you say be simply 'Yes' or 'No'; anything more than this comes from evil."

Matthew 5:37

One of the reasons women often feel overwhelmed is the struggle to say "no." Whether it's fear of disappointing others or the pressure to do it all, overcommitting can quickly lead to burnout. However, Matthew 5:37 reminds you of the importance of being clear and intentional with your commitments.

God has given you the grace to say "no" when something doesn't align with His will or when it threatens to steal your peace. Saying "no" is not selfish; it's an act of wisdom and obedience. It allows you to focus on what

God has called you to do and to protect your time and energy for the people and priorities that matter most.

Learning to say "no" can be challenging, but it is essential for living a life of balance and grace. Trust that God will guide you as you make decisions and honor Him with your time.

- Reflect on your current commitments and evaluate which ones align with God's purpose for you. Practice saying "no" to one request this week to create space for what matters most.

Prayer

Lord, give me the grace to say "no" when needed and the wisdom to discern what aligns with Your will. Help me to let go of guilt and to honor You with my time and energy. Amen.

April 14

Embracing Grace Daily

"Let us then approach God's throne of grace with confidence, so that we may receive mercy and find grace to help us in our time of need."
Hebrews 4:16

God's grace is not a one-time gift; it's something you can access daily. Hebrews 4:16 invites you to approach His throne with confidence, knowing that His mercy and grace are always available to help you in your time of need.

Living under grace means acknowledging your dependence on God and trusting Him to provide everything you need for each day. It means letting go of the pressure to perform or prove yourself and resting in His love and provision.

When you embrace grace, you can face life's challenges with confidence, knowing that God is with you. His grace empowers you to live with peace, joy, and purpose, no matter what comes your way.

- Start each day by thanking God for His grace and asking Him to help you rely on it throughout the day. Keep a journal to record the ways you see His grace at work in your life.

Prayer

Lord, thank You for Your abundant grace that is available to me every day. Help me to rely on Your strength and provision in all I do. Teach me to live with confidence and peace, knowing that You are always with me. Amen.

15

Finding Joy in Everyday Tasks

A pril 25

Seeing Work as Worship

"Whatever you do, work at it with all your heart, as working for the Lord, not for human masters."
Colossians 3:23

The mundane tasks of daily life—cleaning, cooking, running errands—can sometimes feel like a burden. Yet Colossians 3:23 reminds us that every task, no matter how small, can be done for God's glory. When you approach your work with this mindset, even the most ordinary tasks become an act of worship.

Seeing work as worship means shifting your perspective. Instead of focusing on the drudgery, consider how your efforts honor God and bless others. Preparing a meal, for example, becomes an act of love for your family. Tidying your home reflects gratitude for the space God has provided.

By dedicating your tasks to the Lord, you invite His presence into your daily routines. This transforms your work from something mundane into something meaningful, bringing joy and purpose to every moment.

- Start your day by dedicating all your tasks to God. Before beginning a chore, take a moment to thank Him for the opportunity to serve and ask Him to bless your work.

Prayer

Lord, help me to see my daily tasks as acts of worship. Teach me to work with a joyful heart, knowing that everything I do can honor You. Thank You for the opportunity to serve You in the ordinary moments of life. Amen.

April 16

Finding Joy in Serving Others
"Serve one another humbly in love."
Galatians 5:13

It's easy to view everyday tasks as a chore, but when you see them as a way to serve others, they take on new significance. Galatians 5:13 calls us to serve one another in love. This means looking beyond the task itself and focusing on the blessing it brings to those around you.

When you clean your home, cook a meal, or help someone in need, you're not just completing a task—you're expressing love. Serving others doesn't have to be grand or elaborate; it's often in the simple, everyday acts that God's love shines brightest.

Finding joy in serving requires a heart of gratitude and humility. When you serve with love, you reflect Christ's example and experience the joy that comes from putting others before yourself.

- Choose one task today that directly serves someone else—whether it's preparing a special meal, helping with a chore, or offering a kind word. Perform it with love and gratitude.

Prayer

Lord, thank You for the privilege of serving others. Help me to approach each task with a heart of love and humility, knowing that through service, I reflect Your love. Teach me to find joy in blessing those around me. Amen.

April 17

Gratitude in the Ordinary

"Give thanks in all circumstances; for this is God's will for you in Christ Jesus."
1 Thessalonians 5:18

It's easy to overlook the blessings in daily life, especially when tasks feel repetitive or mundane. However, 1 Thessalonians 5:18 encourages you to give thanks in all circumstances—including the ordinary moments. Gratitude shifts your perspective and opens your heart to the joy that God provides.

When you choose gratitude, even simple tasks become opportunities to praise God. Washing dishes can remind you of the meal He provided. Folding laundry can lead you to thank Him for the clothes you wear. Each task becomes a moment to reflect on His goodness.

Gratitude doesn't ignore challenges; it focuses on God's presence and provision in the midst of them. By cultivating a thankful heart, you find joy not in the task itself but in the God who walks with you through it.

- Make a list of things you're grateful for, even in the most mundane aspects of your day. Pause during tasks to thank God for His blessings.

Prayer

Father, thank You for Your abundant blessings, even in the ordinary moments of life. Help me to cultivate a heart of gratitude and to see Your hand at work in everything I do. Teach me to find joy in giving thanks to You. Amen.

April 18

Trusting God with the Details

"Commit to the Lord whatever you do, and He will establish your plans."
Proverbs 16:3

The small, repetitive tasks of life can feel insignificant, but God is deeply involved in every detail of your day. Proverbs 16:3 invites you to commit all your work to Him, trusting that He will guide and bless your efforts.

It's easy to feel overwhelmed by the weight of responsibilities, wondering if what you're doing truly matters. But even the smallest acts, when done in faith, are significant to God. He sees your heart and the love behind your actions. When you commit your work to Him, He brings meaning and purpose to even the simplest tasks.

Trusting God with the details doesn't mean everything will go perfectly. It means acknowledging that He is sovereign and that His plans for you are good. When you place your trust in Him, you can rest in His care, knowing that every effort done for His glory will bear fruit.

- Before starting your daily tasks, pray and commit them to God. Trust Him with the outcomes, even if things don't go as planned. Remind yourself that He values your faithfulness in the little things.

Prayer

Lord, I commit my work to You today. Help me to trust You with every detail and to find joy in knowing that You are with me. Remind me that even the smallest tasks have purpose when done for Your glory. Amen.

April 19

Joy in God's Presence

"You make known to me the path of life; you will fill me with joy in your presence."

Psalm 16:11

Joy isn't found in the completion of tasks but in the presence of God. Psalm 16:11 reminds you that true joy comes from walking with Him. When you invite God into your daily routines, the ordinary becomes extraordinary because He is with you.

Consider how you can experience His presence in the mundane moments of life. As you fold laundry or drive to work, take a moment to thank Him for His faithfulness. Whisper a prayer or reflect on a verse that encourages your heart. These small acts of connection remind you that God is always near, ready to fill your heart with joy.

God's presence transforms your perspective. Instead of viewing your tasks as burdens, you begin to see them as opportunities to honor Him and draw closer to His heart.

- Set reminders throughout your day to pause and acknowledge God's presence. Use moments of stillness to pray or meditate on a verse, inviting His joy into your day.

Prayer

Lord, thank You for the gift of Your presence. Help me to find joy in knowing that You are with me in every moment. Teach me to turn to You throughout my day and to rest in the joy You provide. Amen.

April 20
Working for an Eternal Reward

"And whatever you do, whether in word or deed, do it all in the name of the Lord Jesus."
Colossians 3:17

It's easy to feel like the tasks you do daily are repetitive and insignificant. But Colossians 3:17 reminds you that everything you do can be an offering to God when done in His name. This eternal perspective gives meaning to your work, no matter how small it may seem.

When you work with eternity in mind, you're reminded that God sees and values your efforts. A kind word spoken, a chore completed with love, or a moment spent in prayer—these acts of faithfulness build His kingdom in ways you may not fully understand.

Your reward is not the applause of people but the approval of your Heavenly Father. Knowing that your work has eternal value can bring joy and purpose to every aspect of your day.

- Before starting a task, dedicate it to God and remind yourself that you're working for His glory. Reflect on how your work contributes to His purposes in your life and the lives of others.

Prayer

Father, help me to work with eternity in mind. Remind me that everything I do can bring glory to You when done with a faithful heart. Thank You for the eternal significance You give to even the smallest acts of service. Amen.

April 21

Rejoicing in God's Faithfulness
"The joy of the Lord is your strength."
Nehemiah 8:10

At the end of a busy week, it's easy to feel exhausted or discouraged by what you didn't accomplish. But Nehemiah 8:10 reminds you that the joy of the Lord is your strength. His faithfulness is what sustains you, not your own efforts or accomplishments.

Take time to reflect on how God has been faithful throughout the week. He has provided you with strength for each day, wisdom for your decisions, and grace for your shortcomings. Rejoicing in His faithfulness fills your heart with gratitude and renews your strength for the days ahead.

When you find joy in God's faithfulness, you're reminded that His love and provision are constant. This joy empowers you to keep moving forward, knowing that He is with you every step of the way.

- Set aside time to reflect on the past week and write down specific ways you've seen God's faithfulness in your life. Use this as an opportunity to thank Him and celebrate His goodness.

Prayer

Lord, thank You for Your faithfulness in my life. Help me to find strength in Your joy and to trust that You will continue to sustain me. Teach me to rejoice in Your goodness and to carry that joy into each day. Amen.

16

Managing Expectations with God's Help

April 22

Surrendering Unrealistic Expectations
"Cast all your anxiety on Him because He cares for you."
1 Peter 5:7

Unrealistic expectations often lead to stress and disappointment. You may expect perfection from yourself, others, or even circumstances, only to find that reality falls short. 1 Peter 5:7 reminds you to cast your anxieties—including unmet expectations—on God, trusting that He cares for you.

Letting go of unrealistic expectations begins with surrender. It means acknowledging that you cannot control everything and that perfection is not the goal. God doesn't call you to meet every standard the world imposes; He calls you to rest in His grace and trust in His perfect plan.

When you release your expectations to God, you open the door for His peace to fill your heart. Surrendering doesn't mean settling for less; it means trusting that God's ways are higher than yours and that His plans are always good.

- Identify one unrealistic expectation you've been holding on to. Pray and consciously surrender it to God, asking Him to align your heart

114

with His will.

Prayer

Lord, I release my unrealistic expectations to You. Teach me to trust Your plan and to rest in Your grace. Thank You for caring for me and guiding me through life's uncertainties. Amen.

April 23

Adjusting to God's Timeline

"There is a time for everything, and a season for every activity under the heavens."

Ecclesiastes 3:1

Life doesn't always follow the timeline you envision. You may expect to reach certain milestones by a specific age or see results from your efforts within a set period. When things don't happen as planned, it's easy to feel frustrated or discouraged.

Ecclesiastes 3:1 reminds you that God has a perfect timeline for everything. His timing is not rushed, and it's never delayed. Learning to trust His schedule requires patience and faith, but it also brings freedom. You no longer have to strive to make things happen in your own strength.

Instead of focusing on what hasn't happened, focus on what God is doing in your current season. Trust that He is working behind the scenes, preparing you for what's next. His timing is always worth the wait.

- Write down an area of your life where you're struggling to trust God's timing. Pray daily, asking for patience and faith as you wait for His plan to unfold.

Prayer

Lord, thank You for reminding me that Your timing is perfect. Help me to trust Your plan and to embrace the season I'm in. Give me the patience to wait on You and the faith to believe that You are working for my good. Amen.

April 24

Managing Expectations of Others

"Be completely humble and gentle; be patient, bearing with one another in love."
Ephesians 4:2

People are not perfect, yet it's easy to place high expectations on those closest to you. When others fall short of your expectations, it can lead to frustration, hurt, and strained relationships.

Ephesians 4:2 reminds you to approach others with humility, gentleness, and patience. Managing expectations of others begins with grace—remembering that just as you are imperfect and in need of grace, so are they.

When you let go of unrealistic demands and choose to see others through God's eyes, you open the door for healthier, more loving relationships. Instead of focusing on what someone hasn't done, focus on their strengths and the ways they bless your life.

- Take a moment to reflect on your relationships. Are you holding anyone to unrealistic standards? Practice extending grace by acknowledging their efforts and thanking them for what they do well.

Prayer

Father, help me to manage my expectations of others with humility and grace. Teach me to see people through Your eyes and to love them as You do. Thank You for the relationships You've placed in my life. Amen.

April 25

Releasing Expectations of Yourself

"But He said to me, 'My grace is sufficient for you, for my power is made perfect

in weakness.'"
2 Corinthians 12:9

Many of us hold ourselves to impossibly high standards, striving to do it all and never fall short. But God's grace reminds you that perfection is not required—His strength is made perfect in your weakness.

Releasing unrealistic expectations of yourself means accepting that you're human. You will make mistakes, feel overwhelmed, and fall short at times, but that's where God's grace steps in. He doesn't measure you by your performance; He loves you as His child.

When you let go of the pressure to meet every expectation, you make space for God's strength to shine in your life. Instead of striving, you begin to rely on Him. And in that reliance, you find freedom and joy.

- Identify one area where you're holding yourself to an impossible standard. Write it down and remind yourself that God's grace is enough. Ask Him to help you let go of the pressure and lean on His strength.

Prayer

Lord, I release my unrealistic expectations of myself to You. Thank You for loving me as I am and for giving me the strength to carry out Your purpose. Help me to rely on Your grace and to find joy in my limitations, knowing that You are strong in my weakness. Amen.

April 26

Trusting God When Expectations Are Not Met

"And we know that in all things God works for the good of those who love Him, who have been called according to His purpose."
Romans 8:28

Unmet expectations can be deeply disappointing, whether it's a missed opportunity, a broken dream, or an unforeseen challenge. But Romans

8:28 reminds you that God is always at work, bringing good even out of situations that feel painful or confusing.

Trusting God when expectations are not met requires faith in His character. He is good, faithful, and loving. Even when things don't go as planned, His purposes remain steadfast. While you may not always understand His ways, you can trust that His plans for you are greater than anything you could imagine.

When you release your unmet expectations to God, you invite Him to rewrite your story. In doing so, you discover that His plans are always better than your own.

- Take time to reflect on a recent disappointment. Write it down and pray over it, asking God to help you trust His plan and to show you the good He is bringing through it.

Prayer

Father, thank You for reminding me that You work all things for my good. Help me to trust You when my expectations are not met and to believe that Your plans are always better. Give me peace as I surrender my disappointments to You. Amen.

April 27

Finding Contentment in God's Will

"But godliness with contentment is great gain."
1 Timothy 6:6

Contentment is the antidote to unmet expectations. Instead of striving for what you think should happen, finding joy in God's will allows you to rest in His plans. 1 Timothy 6:6 reminds you that godliness paired with contentment leads to great gain—not in material wealth, but in peace and satisfaction in God.

True contentment comes from trusting that God knows what's best for you. When you focus on His blessings and faithfulness, you find joy in the present instead of longing for what's missing.

Contentment is not complacency. It's an active choice to trust God and embrace His will for your life, even when it doesn't align with your expectations.

- Make a list of things you're grateful for in your current season. Reflect on how these blessings demonstrate God's faithfulness and ask Him to help you cultivate contentment in His will.

Prayer

Lord, thank You for the blessings You've given me. Teach me to be content in Your will and to trust that Your plans are good. Help me to find joy in the present, knowing that You are always with me. Amen.

April 28

Living with Hope for the Future

"For I know the plans I have for you," declares the Lord, "plans to prosper you and not to harm you, plans to give you hope and a future."
Jeremiah 29:11

Managing expectations doesn't mean letting go of hope. Jeremiah 29:11 reminds you that God's plans for your future are filled with hope and purpose. Even when life doesn't go as expected, His promises remain true.

Living with hope means trusting that God is in control of your future. It's about releasing your own limited vision and embracing His greater plan. While you may not see the full picture now, you can trust that He is weaving together something beautiful.

Hope in God sustains you through unmet expectations and challenges. It gives you the courage to keep moving forward, knowing that He holds your future in His hands.

- Take time to pray over your future, asking God to align your desires with His will. Write down one promise from Scripture that gives you hope and keep it visible as a reminder of His faithfulness.

Prayer

Lord, thank You for the hope You give me for the future. Help me to trust Your plans and to live with confidence, knowing that You are in control. Teach me to release my expectations and to embrace the hope found in Your promises. Amen.

V

May: Discovering Your Purpose

17

God's Plan for Your Life

May 1

Trusting God's Sovereignty

"For I know the plans I have for you,' declares the Lord, 'plans to prosper you and not to harm you, plans to give you hope and a future.'"
Jeremiah 29:11

One of the most comforting truths in Scripture is that God has a plan for your life. Jeremiah 29:11 assures you that His plans are for your good, filled with hope and a future. However, trusting God's sovereignty can be challenging, especially when life feels uncertain or overwhelming.

God's plan is not always easy to see, but it is always at work. He knows the end from the beginning, and His wisdom is far greater than ours. Trusting His sovereignty means believing that even when circumstances don't make sense, He is in control and working for your good.

As you trust Him, you'll find peace in knowing that your life is not random. Every step is guided by His loving hand, even when the road ahead seems unclear.

- Take time to reflect on moments when God's plan unfolded in unexpected but good ways in your life. Write these instances down to remind yourself of His faithfulness.

Prayer

Lord, thank You for the plans You have for my life. Help me to trust Your sovereignty, even when I don't understand what You're doing. Give me faith to rest in Your promises and to follow where You lead. Amen.

May 2

Aligning Your Desires with God's Will

"Take delight in the Lord, and He will give you the desires of your heart."
Psalm 37:4

Many people misinterpret Psalm 37:4 to mean that God will grant every wish. But the truth is deeper: when you delight in the Lord, your desires begin to align with His will. He shapes your heart to long for the things that bring Him glory and fulfill His purpose in your life.

Aligning your desires with God's will requires spending time with Him. Through prayer, reading His Word, and seeking His guidance, your heart is transformed. Over time, you'll find that your dreams and goals begin to reflect His priorities rather than your own.

This doesn't mean your unique passions or gifts are ignored. God often uses the talents and dreams He's placed within you as part of His plan. When you align these desires with His will, you'll experience greater fulfillment and joy.

- Spend time in prayer, asking God to align your desires with His will. Write down the passions or dreams on your heart and surrender them to Him, asking for clarity and direction.

Prayer

Father, help me to delight in You and to align my desires with Your will. Shape my heart to long for what pleases You, and guide me as I pursue the plans You have for my life. Amen.

May 3

Trusting the Process

"Being confident of this, that He who began a good work in you will carry it on to completion until the day of Christ Jesus."

Philippians 1:6

God's plan for your life is a process, not an instant result. Philippians 1:6 reminds you that He is faithful to complete the good work He has started in you. This process involves growth, refinement, and sometimes waiting, but it is always leading toward His perfect will.

Trusting the process means believing that God is at work, even when you can't see progress. It means remaining faithful in the small things and trusting that He is using them to prepare you for what's ahead.

When you feel impatient or discouraged, remember that God's timing is perfect. He is not in a hurry, and His plan for your life is unfolding exactly as it should.

- Identify one area of your life where you feel "unfinished." Surrender it to God and commit to trusting Him through the process. Look for small ways He might be working in this season.

Prayer

Lord, thank You for the work You are doing in my life. Help me to trust the process and to remain faithful in every season. Remind me that Your timing is perfect and that You will complete the work You've begun in me. Amen.

May 4

Walking by Faith, Not by Sight

"For we live by faith, not by sight."

2 Corinthians 5:7

God's plan often requires walking by faith rather than relying on what you can see or understand. Trusting Him means stepping out even when the path isn't clear, knowing that He will guide your every step.

Living by faith can be challenging, especially in a world that values certainty and control. But faith is the foundation of your relationship with God. It's trusting that He is with you, even in the unknown.

When you choose to walk by faith, you are declaring that God is bigger than your fears, doubts, or limitations. You are putting your confidence in His ability to lead you, even when you can't see the full picture. Each step of faith brings you closer to His purpose and deepens your relationship with Him.

- Reflect on a situation in your life where you feel unsure or hesitant. Pray for courage to step out in faith and trust God to guide you. Take one small step toward obedience today, even if the outcome is uncertain.

Prayer

Lord, help me to walk by faith and not by sight. Give me the courage to trust You in the unknown and to take steps of obedience, even when the way forward seems unclear. Thank You for guiding me and being with me every step of the way. Amen.

May 5

Finding Purpose in Every Season

"And we know that in all things God works for the good of those who love Him, who have been called according to His purpose."
Romans 8:28

Every season of life has a purpose, even the challenging or unexpected ones. Romans 8:28 assures you that God is working all things for your good and

His glory, weaving every experience into His greater plan.

It's easy to feel discouraged in seasons of waiting, loss, or difficulty. But these times are not wasted. God uses them to refine your character, draw you closer to Him, and prepare you for what's next.

Trusting God's purpose in every season requires a shift in perspective. Instead of asking, "Why is this happening?" ask, "How can I grow through this?" When you trust that God is at work, you can find peace and meaning, even in life's hardest moments.

- Think about your current season of life. Write down one way God might be working in or through you during this time. Ask Him to help you embrace His purpose and trust His plan for this season.

Prayer

Father, thank You for working all things for my good. Help me to see Your purpose in this season of my life and to trust that You are in control. Teach me to grow and to rely on You as You prepare me for what's ahead. Amen.

May 6

Staying Committed to God's Plan

"Commit to the Lord whatever you do, and He will establish your plans."
Proverbs 16:3

Commitment to God's plan requires surrender and trust. Proverbs 16:3 encourages you to commit your actions and decisions to the Lord, trusting that He will guide your steps and establish your path.

Staying committed isn't always easy. You may encounter setbacks, delays, or temptations to follow your own way. But when you trust God and prioritize His plan, He will lead you toward the purpose He has for your life.

Commitment also means aligning your daily choices with His will. It's about seeking His guidance in every decision, big or small, and trusting that He knows what's best for you. When you stay committed to God's plan, you'll find stability and direction, even in uncertain times.

- Choose one area of your life where you want to deepen your commitment to God's plan. Pray for wisdom and take a practical step toward aligning that area with His will today.

Prayer

Lord, I commit my plans and actions to You. Help me to stay faithful to Your purpose and to trust You in every decision. Thank You for guiding me and establishing my steps as I follow You. Amen.

May 7
Embracing God's Ultimate Purpose
"For it is God who works in you to will and to act in order to fulfill His good purpose."
Philippians 2:13

God's ultimate purpose for your life is to bring Him glory and to reflect His love to the world. Philippians 2:13 reminds you that He is working in you, equipping you to fulfill His good purpose.

Embracing God's purpose means focusing on His kingdom rather than your own. It's about seeking opportunities to serve others, share His love, and live in a way that honors Him. When you align your life with His ultimate purpose, you'll find true fulfillment and joy.

God's purpose is not just about what you do; it's about who you are becoming. As you grow in your relationship with Him, He transforms your heart and equips you to live out His plan.

- Reflect on how you can live out God's purpose in your daily life. Identify one way you can serve or show His love to someone today.

Prayer

Father, thank You for working in me to fulfill Your good purpose. Help me to live in a way that glorifies You and reflects Your love to the world. Equip me to follow Your plan and to trust that Your purpose for my life is always good. Amen.

18

Serving Others with a Joyful Heart

M^{ay 8}

The Call to Serve

"For even the Son of Man did not come to be served, but to serve, and to give His life as a ransom for many."

Mark 10:45

Jesus, the Son of God, exemplified a life of service. He didn't come to demand attention or recognition but to humbly serve others and give His life for humanity. This is the same call He places on your life—to serve others as a reflection of His love and grace.

Serving others is not always convenient or glamorous. It can mean sacrificing your time, energy, and resources. However, when you serve with a joyful heart, you align yourself with Jesus' mission and become a conduit of His love to the world.

God's call to serve is not limited to specific roles or positions. It's found in the small, everyday acts of kindness and generosity. Whether it's helping a neighbor, encouraging a friend, or volunteering in your community, every act of service matters in God's kingdom.

• Look for one simple way to serve someone today, whether it's offering a helping hand, a kind word, or a listening ear. Reflect on how this act reflects God's love to the world.

Prayer

Lord, thank You for the example of Jesus, who came to serve and not to be served. Teach me to follow His example and to serve others with a joyful heart. Help me to see opportunities to show Your love through my actions. Amen.

May 9

Serving with Humility

"Do nothing out of selfish ambition or vain conceit. Rather, in humility value others above yourselves."

Philippians 2:3

True service begins with humility. It's about putting others before yourself and valuing their needs and well-being. Philippians 2:3 challenges you to serve not out of selfish ambition but with a heart focused on honoring God and uplifting others.

Humility in service means recognizing that every act, no matter how small, is significant in God's eyes. It's not about seeking recognition or praise but about reflecting Christ's love. Serving with humility can also mean letting go of pride and being willing to do tasks that seem unnoticed or unimportant.

When you serve with humility, you mirror Jesus' attitude, who humbled Himself to serve humanity, even to the point of death on the cross.

- Identify an opportunity to serve in a way that may go unnoticed or unappreciated. Do it joyfully and without seeking acknowledgment, knowing that God sees and values your humility.

Prayer

Father, help me to serve with humility, valuing others above myself. Teach me to follow Jesus' example and to find joy in serving for Your glory rather than for recognition. Thank You for the opportunity to reflect Your love through my actions. Amen.

May 10

Finding Joy in Serving

"Serve the Lord with gladness! Come into His presence with singing!"
Psalm 100:2

Serving others is not a burden but a privilege. Psalm 100:2 reminds you to serve the Lord with gladness, knowing that every act of service is an opportunity to glorify Him and spread His love.

Joy in serving comes when you shift your focus from yourself to God. Instead of viewing service as an obligation, see it as an act of worship. When your heart is aligned with His, even the most mundane tasks become meaningful.

The joy of serving is rooted in the impact it has on others and the fulfillment it brings to your soul. As you pour out love, kindness, and generosity, you reflect God's character and draw closer to Him.

- Choose one act of service to perform today, and do it with intentional joy. Reflect on how this act brings glory to God and blesses those around you.

Prayer

Lord, thank You for the joy that comes from serving You and others. Help me to see service as an act of worship and to perform every task with gladness. May my actions reflect Your love and bring glory to Your name. Amen.

May 11

Serving in Love

"Serve one another humbly in love." Galatians 5:13

Service motivated by love reflects the heart of Christ. Galatians 5:13 reminds you that serving others is not about obligation or duty but about showing God's love in action. When love is the foundation of your service, it becomes a powerful testimony of your faith.

Love-driven service means seeing others as God sees them—valued and worthy of care. It involves patience, compassion, and selflessness, even when it's inconvenient or unnoticed. This kind of service mirrors Christ's love, who gave His life for you out of His deep love for humanity.

Serving in love also transforms relationships and communities. It brings healing, encouragement, and hope to those who receive it. And as you serve with love, you grow closer to God, reflecting His nature in your daily life.

- Identify one person who could use an extra dose of love today. Serve them in a way that shows care and compassion—whether through a kind gesture, a note of encouragement, or simply spending time with them.

Prayer

Lord, fill my heart with Your love so I may serve others humbly and joyfully. Teach me to reflect Your compassion and care in all I do. Let my service point others to Your grace and goodness. Amen.

May 12

Persevering in Service

"Let us not become weary in doing good, for at the proper time we will reap a harvest if we do not give up."
Galatians 6:9

Serving others can sometimes feel exhausting, especially when it seems like your efforts go unnoticed or unappreciated. Galatians 6:9 encourages you to persevere, trusting that your service has eternal value and that God will reward your faithfulness in His perfect timing.

Perseverance in service means staying committed, even when it's hard. It's about remembering that you are ultimately serving God, not people. When you focus on His purpose and rely on His strength, you can find renewed energy and joy to keep going.

God sees your efforts, even when others don't. He is faithful to bless your work and use it to accomplish His plans. Trust that every act of service, no matter how small, is part of a greater harvest that He is preparing.

- If you're feeling weary in service, take time to pray and ask God for renewed strength. Reflect on why you serve and remind yourself of the impact your actions have on others and for God's kingdom.

Prayer

Lord, help me to persevere in serving others, even when it's difficult. Renew my strength and remind me of the eternal purpose in my efforts. Thank You for the promise of a harvest and for Your faithfulness in using my service for Your glory. Amen.

May 13

Using Your Gifts to Serve

"Each of you should use whatever gift you have received to serve others, as faithful stewards of God's grace in its various forms."
1 Peter 4:10

God has uniquely gifted you to serve others and bring glory to Him. Whether your talents are creative, practical, relational, or spiritual, they are given to you as tools to reflect His grace and love.

Using your gifts to serve doesn't have to be complicated. It's about recognizing the unique ways God has equipped you and finding opportunities to use those abilities for His kingdom. Whether you're good at teaching, encouraging, organizing, or helping, your contributions are valuable and essential.

When you use your gifts in service to others, you're not only blessing them but also honoring God as a faithful steward of what He has entrusted to you.

- Take time to identify your gifts and how you can use them to serve others. Consider volunteering in your church, community, or another area where your talents can make a difference.

Prayer

Father, thank You for the unique gifts You've given me. Show me how to use them to serve others and glorify You. Help me to be a faithful steward of what You've entrusted to me, using my abilities to reflect Your grace. Amen.

May 14

Serving as Worship

"Whatever you do, work at it with all your heart, as working for the Lord, not for human masters."
Colossians 3:23

When you view service as an act of worship, it transforms even the simplest tasks into meaningful offerings to God. Colossians 3:23 reminds you to work with all your heart, not for human approval but to honor the Lord.

Serving as worship means approaching every task with gratitude and dedication, knowing that God is glorified through your efforts. It's not about perfection or recognition but about offering your best to Him out of love and reverence.

This perspective brings joy and purpose to your service. Whether you're caring for your family, helping a friend, or volunteering in your community, every act becomes an opportunity to worship and reflect God's love.

- Choose one task today—big or small—and dedicate it to God as an act of worship. Perform it with gratitude and excellence, focusing on honoring Him through your efforts.

Prayer

Lord, teach me to serve as an act of worship. Help me to approach every task with gratitude and joy, offering my best to You. Thank You for the privilege of serving others and reflecting Your love through my actions. Amen.

19

Walking in Confidence and Calling

May 15

Confidence in God's Purpose

"For we are God's handiwork, created in Christ Jesus to do good works, which God prepared in advance for us to do."
Ephesians 2:10

God has a unique purpose for your life. You were created intentionally, crafted by His hands, and equipped to fulfill the good works He prepared for you. This truth should fill you with confidence—not in yourself but in the One who made you and called you according to His plans.

It's easy to feel uncertain or inadequate when faced with challenges or expectations. But your confidence doesn't have to come from your abilities or achievements. Instead, it comes from knowing that God has called you and will equip you to fulfill His purpose.

Walking in confidence requires trust in God's sovereignty. He knows your strengths and weaknesses, and He will use them for His glory. Remember, your worth and calling are not dependent on what others say or think but on God's unchanging truth about who you are in Him.

• Take a moment to reflect on your strengths and passions. Write them down and pray for God's guidance on how you can use them to walk in His purpose.

Prayer

Father, thank You for creating me with a purpose. Help me to trust in Your plan and to walk confidently in the calling You have placed on my life. May my confidence always be rooted in Your truth and not in my own abilities. Amen.

May 16

Overcoming Fear and Doubt

"For the Spirit God gave us does not make us timid, but gives us power, love, and self-discipline."

2 Timothy 1:7

Fear and doubt can hold you back from fully embracing your calling. They whisper lies that you're not enough, that you'll fail, or that someone else is better suited for the task. But God's Word reminds you that He has given you a spirit of power, love, and self-discipline—not fear or timidity.

When fear creeps in, remember who God is. He is your strength and your shield, equipping you to face challenges with courage. Walking in your calling doesn't mean you won't feel fear, but it does mean you don't have to let it control you.

Doubt often arises when you focus on your limitations instead of God's power. Shift your perspective by meditating on His promises and trusting that He will provide what you need. When you step out in faith, you'll see that He is faithful to guide and sustain you.

- Identify one fear or doubt that's holding you back. Write down a scripture that speaks to that fear, and pray for God's help in overcoming it. Take a small step of faith toward your calling today.

Prayer

Lord, thank You for giving me a spirit of power, love, and self-discipline. Help me to overcome fear and doubt, trusting in Your strength and provision. Remind me that You are always with me as I walk in my calling. Amen.

May 17

Trusting God with Your Calling

"Trust in the Lord with all your heart and lean not on your own understanding; in all your ways submit to Him, and He will make your paths straight."

Proverbs 3:5-6

Walking in your calling requires complete trust in God. He knows the path ahead, even when you can't see it. Trusting Him means submitting your plans and desires to His will, believing that His ways are higher and better than your own.

Sometimes, your calling may feel unclear or overwhelming. You may wonder if you're on the right path or question whether you're capable of fulfilling God's purpose. In these moments, remember that He is faithful to lead and guide you. Your role is to take each step in obedience, trusting that He will make your paths straight.

When you trust God with your calling, you can walk forward with peace and confidence, knowing that He is in control. His timing is perfect, and His plans for you are good.

- Spend time in prayer, asking God to reveal any areas where you're struggling to trust Him. Surrender your plans to Him and ask for His guidance as you walk in your calling.

Prayer

Lord, I trust You with my calling and my future. Help me to lean on You and not my own understanding. Guide my steps and give me the confidence to follow Your plan, knowing that You are faithful and good. Amen.

May 18

Embracing Your Identity in Christ

"But you are a chosen people, a royal priesthood, a holy nation, God's special possession, that you may declare the praises of Him who called you out of darkness into His wonderful light."
1 Peter 2:9

Understanding your identity in Christ is foundational to walking confidently in your calling. You are not defined by your past mistakes, shortcomings, or what others think of you. Instead, you are defined by who God says you are: chosen, loved, and called for a purpose.

Embracing this identity means walking in the knowledge that you belong to God and that He has set you apart to declare His goodness. This truth frees you from striving for approval or feeling unworthy. Your confidence doesn't come from your abilities but from the assurance that God's power is working through you.

As you embrace your identity in Christ, you'll find that your calling becomes clearer. It's not about what you do, but about who you are in Him and how you reflect His light in the world.

- Take a moment to write down affirmations based on 1 Peter 2:9 (e.g., "I am chosen," "I am God's special possession"). Speak these truths over yourself daily to remind you of your identity in Christ.

Prayer

Lord, thank You for choosing me and calling me Your own. Help me to walk in the confidence of my identity in You. Let my life reflect Your goodness and light to those around me. Amen.

May 19

Walking in Obedience

"If you are willing and obedient, you will eat the good things of the land."
Isaiah 1:19

Obedience to God is a key part of fulfilling your calling. It's not always easy, especially when His plans don't align with your own or when the path ahead seems uncertain. However, obedience brings blessing and positions you to experience God's best for your life.

Walking in obedience means saying "yes" to God even when it's uncomfortable or inconvenient. It means trusting Him enough to follow His lead, knowing that His ways are higher than yours. As you take steps of faith in obedience, you'll see how He works through your willingness to accomplish His purposes.

Obedience also requires a heart that is fully surrendered to God. It's about aligning your will with His and being open to His guidance in every area of your life. When you walk in obedience, you'll find that His blessings and provision follow.

- Identify one area in your life where you feel God calling you to obedience. Take a step of faith today, trusting that He will guide and bless your decision.

Prayer

Lord, help me to walk in obedience to Your will. Give me the courage to say "yes" to Your plans, even when it's hard. Thank You for the blessings that come from following You. Amen.

May 20

Walking Boldly in Faith

"So we say with confidence, 'The Lord is my helper; I will not be afraid. What can mere mortals do to me?'"
Hebrews 13:6

Walking in confidence and calling requires bold faith. It means stepping out even when you don't have all the answers or when challenges arise. Bold faith is not the absence of fear but choosing to trust God's promises over your circumstances.

Hebrews 13:6 reminds you that the Lord is your helper, so you have no reason to fear. When you place your confidence in Him, you can face any situation with courage and assurance. God's power is made perfect in your weakness, and His strength enables you to walk boldly in your calling.

Bold faith also inspires others. When people see your confidence in God, it encourages them to trust Him in their own lives. Your willingness to step out in faith can have a ripple effect, drawing others closer to Him.

- Take a bold step toward your calling today, whether it's starting a new project, having a difficult conversation, or pursuing a dream God has placed on your heart. Trust Him to guide and provide.

Prayer

Lord, thank You for being my helper and my strength. Help me to walk boldly in faith, trusting in Your promises and power. Use my confidence in You to inspire and encourage others. Amen.

May 21

Living Out Your Calling

"I press on toward the goal to win the prize for which God has called me heavenward in Christ Jesus."
Philippians 3:14

Living out your calling is a lifelong journey. It requires perseverance, focus, and a heart fixed on Christ. Paul's words in Philippians 3:14 remind you to press on, keeping your eyes on the ultimate prize—eternity with God and the fulfillment of His purpose for your life.

Your calling is not just about what you do but about who you become in

Christ. It's about growing in faith, serving others, and bringing glory to God in all that you do. Some days will be harder than others, but God's grace is sufficient to carry you through.

Living out your calling also means being faithful in the small things. Every moment is an opportunity to reflect God's love and to fulfill His purpose, no matter how ordinary it may seem.

- Take time to evaluate how you are living out your calling. Are there areas where you need to refocus or press on? Commit to faithfully pursuing God's purpose in both big and small ways.

Prayer

Lord, thank You for calling me to live a life that glorifies You. Help me to press on with perseverance and focus, trusting in Your strength and grace. Use my life to fulfill Your purpose and reflect Your love. Amen.

20

Trusting God's Timing for Your Dreams

May 22
God's Perfect Timing
"He has made everything beautiful in its time. He has also set eternity in the human heart; yet no one can fathom what God has done from beginning to end."
Ecclesiastes 3:11

Trusting God's timing requires faith in His sovereignty. Ecclesiastes 3:11 reminds you that God has a plan for everything, and He makes things beautiful in His perfect time. However, waiting can often feel challenging, especially when your dreams seem delayed or out of reach.

God's timing is not about convenience but about what is best for you and His greater plan. His perspective is eternal, and He knows what you need and when you need it. While you may feel tempted to rush ahead, trusting His timing teaches patience, builds character, and strengthens your relationship with Him.

As you wait on God's timing, rest in the assurance that He sees you, hears your prayers, and is working behind the scenes. Trust that His plans are good and that He will bring your dreams to fruition in a way that glorifies Him and blesses you.

- Reflect on an area of your life where you're waiting on God. Write a prayer surrendering your timeline to Him and asking for trust in His perfect timing.

Prayer

Lord, thank You for Your perfect timing. Help me to trust that You are making everything beautiful in its time. Teach me patience and strengthen my faith as I wait on You. Amen.

May 23

Trusting God When the Wait Feels Long

"Wait for the Lord; be strong and take heart and wait for the Lord."
Psalm 27:14

Waiting on God can feel discouraging, especially when you're unsure of what lies ahead. Psalm 27:14 encourages you to take heart and be strong in the waiting. The wait is not wasted; it is a time for preparation, growth, and deepening your trust in God.

God often uses the waiting season to shape your character and refine your faith. It's in these moments that you learn to rely on His strength and not your own. While the wait may be uncomfortable, it is a vital part of His process for bringing your dreams to life.

Remember, waiting is not inactivity. It's an opportunity to draw closer to God, to pray, and to prepare for what's to come. Trust that He is working all things together for your good, even when the wait feels long.

- Choose one thing you can do today to prepare for the dream you're waiting on. It could be gaining a skill, deepening your prayer life, or seeking wise counsel.

Prayer

Lord, help me to be strong and take heart as I wait for You. Remind me that the waiting season is part of Your plan. Prepare my heart and equip me for the dreams You have placed in me. Amen.

May 24

Letting Go of Control

"Commit to the Lord whatever you do, and He will establish your plans."
Proverbs 16:3

Letting go of control and trusting God with your dreams can feel daunting. Proverbs 16:3 reminds you to commit your plans to the Lord, trusting that He will guide and establish them according to His purpose.

When you hold on tightly to your own timeline or expectations, it can lead to frustration and anxiety. Surrendering control to God is an act of faith, acknowledging that He knows what's best. His wisdom far surpasses yours, and His plans are always for your good.

As you release control, you open the door for God to work in ways you could never imagine. Surrender doesn't mean giving up on your dreams; it means trusting that God will fulfill them in His perfect way and time.

- Spend time in prayer, asking God to help you release control over your dreams. Write down any worries or expectations you need to surrender, and commit them to Him.

Prayer

Father, I surrender my dreams and plans to You. Help me to let go of control and trust in Your wisdom and timing. Thank You for the promise that You will establish my plans when I commit them to You. Amen.

May 25

Finding Joy in the Waiting

"Be joyful in hope, patient in affliction, faithful in prayer."
Romans 12:12

The waiting season doesn't have to be filled with frustration or discouragement. Romans 12:12 encourages you to find joy in hope, be patient in the process, and remain faithful in prayer. These attitudes transform waiting into a season of purpose and growth.

Joy in the waiting comes from trusting God's promises and knowing that He is faithful. Instead of focusing on what hasn't happened yet, choose to celebrate the blessings in your life and the ways God is working even now.

Patience in affliction means enduring the challenges of waiting with grace and faith. Faithfulness in prayer keeps your heart aligned with God, allowing Him to guide you and give you peace.

- Start a gratitude journal to focus on God's blessings in your life. Each day, write down three things you're thankful for as a reminder of His faithfulness.

Prayer

Lord, help me to find joy in the hope of Your promises. Teach me to be patient in the waiting and faithful in prayer. Thank You for the ways You are working in my life, even when I can't see it. Amen.

May 26

God's Faithfulness in Delays

"The Lord is not slow in keeping His promise, as some understand slowness. Instead, He is patient with you, not wanting anyone to perish, but everyone to come to repentance."

2 Peter 3:9

Delays in fulfilling your dreams can feel disheartening, but they are not a sign of God's neglect. Instead, they are often an expression of His faithfulness and patience. 2 Peter 3:9 reminds you that God operates on a different timeline, always with your best interests at heart.

Delays allow God to work in unseen ways, aligning circumstances, preparing your heart, and building your character. During these times, it's essential to remember that His promises are sure. What may seem like a delay to you is part of His perfect plan.

Rather than focusing on what feels like a setback, use this time to trust in God's goodness and reflect on His faithfulness in the past. He has brought you this far, and He will carry you through.

- Reflect on past situations where God's timing proved better than your own. Write down how His faithfulness was evident, even during delays, and use it as encouragement for your current season of waiting.

Prayer

Father, thank You for Your faithfulness, even in times of delay. Help me to trust that Your timing is perfect and that You are working all things for my good. Strengthen my faith and remind me of Your promises. Amen.

May 27

Trusting God for the Impossible

"Jesus looked at them and said, 'With man this is impossible, but with God all things are possible.'"
Matthew 19:26

Sometimes, your dreams may seem impossible to achieve. The obstacles might feel too big, or the resources might appear too limited. Yet Matthew 19:26 reminds you that nothing is impossible with God. He is the Creator of the universe, the One who parted the sea, and the One who raised the dead.

Trusting God for the impossible requires faith that goes beyond what you can see or understand. It means believing that He is able to do immeasurably more than you could ask or imagine. Your role is to trust and obey, even when the path seems unclear.

God specializes in making the impossible possible. When you place your dreams in His hands, you invite Him to work in ways that bring Him glory and fulfill His purpose for your life.

- Identify a dream or situation in your life that feels impossible. Surrender it to God in prayer and take one small step of faith, trusting Him to do what only He can do.

Prayer

Lord, thank You for being the God of the impossible. Help me to trust You with the dreams that feel out of reach. Strengthen my faith and remind me that nothing is too hard for You. Amen.

May 28

Living in Expectation

"Blessed is she who has believed that the Lord would fulfill His promises to her!"
Luke 1:45

Living in expectation means believing wholeheartedly that God will fulfill His promises. Like Mary in Luke 1:45, you are blessed when you trust in His faithfulness and walk confidently in the assurance of His Word.

This doesn't mean you'll always know how or when God will act, but it means living with hope and anticipation. Expectation is an act of faith that honors God, showing that you trust Him to do what He has said.

As you live in expectation, continue to align your heart with His will through prayer, worship, and obedience. Your hope in God will not disappoint because He is faithful to fulfill His promises in His perfect time.

- Write down a promise from God's Word that speaks to your current dreams. Keep it somewhere visible and read it daily, declaring your trust in His faithfulness.

Prayer

Father, thank You for Your promises and Your faithfulness. Help me to live in expectation, trusting that You will fulfill Your Word in Your perfect timing. Strengthen my faith and fill my heart with hope as I wait on You. Amen.

VI

June: Healing and Restoration

21

Trusting God in Emotional Pain

J**une 1**

God Understands Your Pain

"The Lord is close to the brokenhearted and saves those who are crushed in spirit."

Psalm 34:18

When you are in the midst of emotional pain, it can feel isolating and overwhelming. But Psalm 34:18 assures you that God is near to the brokenhearted. He is not distant from your suffering but walks with you in the darkest valleys of your life.

God understands your pain because He experienced it Himself. Jesus wept at the loss of a friend, felt rejection from His own people, and endured betrayal by those closest to Him. Knowing this can bring comfort, as it means He fully empathizes with your struggles.

Trusting God in emotional pain means bringing your hurt to Him, trusting that He sees your tears and hears your cries. His presence provides comfort, His Word gives hope, and His Spirit strengthens you to face each day.

• Spend time in prayer today, pouring out your emotions to God. Be

153

honest about your pain, and allow His presence to bring comfort. Meditate on Psalm 34:18, repeating it to yourself whenever you feel overwhelmed.

Prayer

Lord, thank You for being close to me when I am brokenhearted. Help me to trust that You see my pain and are working to heal me. Thank You for understanding my struggles and walking with me. Amen.

June 2

God Heals the Brokenhearted

"He heals the brokenhearted and binds up their wounds."
Psalm 147:3

Emotional pain can leave you feeling shattered, but God is the ultimate healer of broken hearts. Psalm 147:3 reminds you that He not only sees your wounds but actively works to bind and heal them.

God's healing doesn't always come instantly, but it is always intentional. He uses time, His Word, and often the love of others to bring restoration to your soul. Emotional pain may seem unbearable, but His healing power is greater.

As you allow God to heal your heart, you may find that He brings beauty from your pain. The experiences that once hurt you deeply can become the foundation for your testimony, encouraging others to find hope in Him.

- Reflect on areas of your life where you need healing. Write them down and surrender them to God in prayer. Seek out Scriptures that speak to His healing power and meditate on them.

Prayer

Father, thank You for being the healer of my heart. I surrender my pain to You and trust You to restore me. Help me to find hope in Your promises and strength in Your love. Amen.

June 3

Finding Peace in the Storm

"Peace I leave with you; my peace I give you. I do not give to you as the world gives. Do not let your hearts be troubled and do not be afraid."
John 14:27

Emotional pain often feels like a storm raging within you, but Jesus promises a peace that transcends circumstances. This peace isn't dependent on external conditions but comes from His presence within you.

Trusting God in emotional pain means leaning into His peace, even when your heart feels heavy. It's a peace that assures you He is in control, that He loves you deeply, and that He will never leave you.

Jesus offers this peace freely, but you must choose to accept it. By focusing on His promises rather than your pain, you can experience calm in the midst of chaos.

Practical Application:

Whenever you feel overwhelmed by emotional pain, take a moment to pause and pray. Ask God to fill you with His peace, and spend time meditating on John 14:27. Consider listening to worship music to refocus your heart.

Prayer

Lord, thank You for the gift of Your peace. Help me to trust You in the midst of my pain and to rest in the assurance of Your love. Calm the storm within me and fill my heart with Your presence. Amen.

June 4

Hope for the Hurting

"Why, my soul, are you downcast? Why so disturbed within me? Put your hope in God, for I will yet praise Him, my Savior and my God." Psalm 42:11

Emotional pain can leave you feeling hopeless, but Psalm 42:11 reminds you to put your hope in God. He is your Savior, your strength, and the One who will carry you through every trial.

Hope is not denying your pain but choosing to trust that God is greater. It's a confidence that He will redeem your circumstances and bring joy from sorrow. Even when your emotions feel overwhelming, hope reminds you that better days are ahead.

As you cling to hope, praise becomes a powerful weapon. Praising God in the midst of pain shifts your focus from your struggles to His greatness, renewing your strength and lifting your spirit.

- Make a list of God's promises that bring hope. them nearby and refer to them whenever you feel downcast. Commit to praising God daily, even if it's as simple as thanking Him for one thing.

Prayer

Father, thank You for being my source of hope. Help me to trust in Your goodness and faithfulness, even when life feels heavy. I choose to praise You, knowing that You will bring beauty from my pain. Amen.

June 5

Casting Your Burdens on God

"Cast all your anxiety on Him because He cares for you."
1 Peter 5:7

Emotional pain often feels like a heavy burden, weighing you down and making it difficult to move forward. But 1 Peter 5:7 reminds you that you don't have to carry it alone. God invites you to cast all your cares and anxieties on Him because He loves you deeply and cares for every detail of your life.

Casting your burdens on God requires surrender. It means trusting Him enough to give Him your pain, your worries, and your fears, believing that He can handle them far better than you can. This act of surrender doesn't mean your pain will instantly disappear, but it does mean you'll no longer face it alone.

God's care is constant and personal. When you bring your burdens to Him, you allow His love and strength to sustain you. Trust that He is working in the background, even when you can't see it, and that He will bring healing in His perfect time.

- Take a moment today to pray and visualize handing your burdens over to God. Write down the specific emotions or situations you're struggling with, and symbolically "give" them to Him by tearing up or discarding the paper after prayer.

Prayer

Lord, thank You for inviting me to cast my burdens on You. Help me to surrender my pain and trust in Your care. Remind me that I am never alone and that Your love is greater than anything I face. Amen.

June 6
Finding Strength in Weakness

"But He said to me, 'My grace is sufficient for you, for My power is made perfect in weakness.' Therefore I will boast all the more gladly about my weaknesses, so that Christ's power may rest on me."

2 Corinthians 12:9

In the midst of emotional pain, it's natural to feel weak and vulnerable. But God's response to your weakness is His abundant grace. 2 Corinthians 12:9 reminds you that His power is made perfect in your moments of weakness, offering strength beyond your own abilities.

Instead of hiding your struggles, bring them to God and allow Him to work through them. Your weakness is not a limitation but an opportunity for His power to shine. When you trust in His grace, you can find strength to face even the most difficult challenges.

Emotional pain may leave you feeling depleted, but God's grace is sufficient. It is an ever-present source of renewal, lifting you up and carrying you forward. Lean into His strength, knowing that He is more than enough for whatever you're facing.

- When you feel overwhelmed by emotional pain, pause and declare God's sufficiency over your situation. Meditate on 2 Corinthians 12:9 and ask for His strength to be made perfect in your weakness.

Prayer

Father, thank You for Your grace that is sufficient for me. In my weakness, I rely on Your strength. Remind me that Your power is made perfect in my struggles, and help me to trust in Your provision. Amen.

June 7

Trusting God to Redeem Your Pain

"And we know that in all things God works for the good of those who love Him, who have been called according to His purpose."
Romans 8:28

Emotional pain can feel purposeless, but Romans 8:28 offers a profound truth: God works all things together for good, even the painful parts of your life. While the pain itself may not be good, God's redemptive power ensures that He can bring beauty from ashes.

Trusting God to redeem your pain means believing that He is always at work, even when you don't understand His plan. It means looking beyond your circumstances and focusing on His character—His goodness, faithfulness, and love.

Redemption doesn't erase your pain but transforms it. God can use your experiences to strengthen your faith, deepen your empathy for others, and glorify His name. Trust Him to bring purpose to your pain and to use it for His glory and your growth.

- Reflect on areas of pain in your life where you need to trust God for redemption. Write a prayer of surrender, asking Him to bring beauty and purpose from your struggles.

Prayer

Lord, thank You for Your promise to work all things together for good. I trust You to redeem my pain and bring purpose to my struggles. Help me to see Your hand at work and to trust in Your plan, even when I don't understand it. Amen.

22

Overcoming Past Hurts

J**une 8**

Acknowledging Your Pain

"You desire truth in the inward parts, and in the hidden part You will make me to know wisdom."

Psalm 51:6

Healing from past hurts begins with acknowledging them. Psalm 51:6 reminds you that God desires honesty in your heart. Denying or suppressing your pain may feel easier, but it prevents true healing.

God already knows your wounds, and He lovingly invites you to bring them to Him. Acknowledging your pain doesn't mean dwelling on it, but it allows you to face it with God's help. Only when you confront your struggles can His wisdom guide you toward healing.

Your pain matters to God. He cares deeply about your heart and wants to see you whole. Be truthful with yourself and with Him about the areas that need His touch.

- Spend time in prayer, asking God to reveal any hidden pain or unresolved hurt in your heart. Journal about how these hurts have impacted you and surrender them to God.

Prayer

Father, thank You for desiring truth in my heart. Help me to face my pain honestly and trust You to guide me toward healing. Bring wisdom to the areas I struggle to understand. Amen.

June 9

Bringing Your Hurts to God

"Come to Me, all you who are weary and burdened, and I will give you rest."
Matthew 11:28

Carrying the weight of past hurts can leave you weary and burdened. Matthew 11:28 is a beautiful invitation from Jesus to bring those burdens to Him. He doesn't promise to erase the pain immediately but offers you rest and peace as you trust Him.

Healing requires vulnerability. When you bring your hurts to God, you allow Him to work in your heart. He is a safe refuge who listens without judgment and comforts without condemnation.

God's rest is not just physical; it is a deep peace for your soul. Trust Him to carry what you cannot and to lead you step by step toward healing and restoration.

- In prayer, imagine placing your burdens into Jesus' hands. Speak openly about the hurts you're carrying and ask Him for rest and peace in your heart.

Prayer

Lord, thank You for inviting me to come to You with my burdens. I lay my hurts at Your feet and trust You to bring rest to my weary soul. Help me to feel Your peace and comfort today. Amen.

June 10

Forgiveness as a Path to Healing

"Be kind and compassionate to one another, forgiving each other, just as in Christ
God forgave you."
Ephesians 4:32

Forgiveness is a powerful step in overcoming past hurts. While it may not erase the pain, it releases the hold that bitterness and resentment have on your heart. Ephesians 4:32 reminds you to forgive others as Christ has forgiven you.

Forgiveness is not about excusing wrongdoing but about freeing yourself from the burden of anger and bitterness. It's an act of grace that mirrors the grace God has shown you.

When you choose forgiveness, you open the door for healing. It may not be easy, but God's Spirit will empower you to forgive, even when it feels impossible.

- Reflect on any lingering unforgiveness in your heart. Pray for the strength to release it to God and take one step toward forgiving those who have hurt you.

Prayer

Father, thank You for forgiving me through Christ. Help me to extend that same forgiveness to others, even when it's hard. Heal my heart as I release bitterness and trust You to bring justice and peace. Amen.

June 11

Releasing the Past

"Forget the former things; do not dwell on the past. See, I am doing a new thing!"
Isaiah 43:18-19

Holding onto past hurts can keep you trapped in a cycle of pain. Isaiah 43:18-19 encourages you to let go of the former things and make room for the new work God wants to do in your life.

Releasing the past doesn't mean forgetting it completely, but it does mean choosing not to let it define you. God's plans for you are full of hope and renewal. When you let go of old wounds, you create space for Him to do something new.

Trust that God is working to bring beauty from your pain. Focus on His promises for the future rather than the disappointments of the past.

- Write down the areas of your life where you feel stuck in past hurts. Pray for God to help you release them and declare His promise of renewal over your life.

Prayer

Lord, thank You for the new things You are doing in my life. Help me to release the past and trust in Your plans for my future. Bring healing and hope as I walk forward in faith. Amen.

June 12

Trusting God to Redeem Your Pain

"And we know that in all things God works for the good of those who love Him, who have been called according to His purpose."

Romans 8:28

The wounds of your past may feel irredeemable, but God specializes in turning pain into purpose. Romans 8:28 reassures you that God is working all things together for your good—even the parts of your story that seem broken.

Trusting God to redeem your pain doesn't mean pretending it didn't happen or minimizing its impact. Instead, it's about believing that He can bring beauty from the ashes. He can transform your experiences into tools of growth, compassion, and testimony.

This redemption process may not happen overnight, and it may not look the way you expect. But as you surrender your pain to Him, you can trust that He will weave it into a greater story of hope and healing.

- Take time to reflect on how God has worked through difficult situations in the past. Journal about how He has brought growth or good from those experiences. If you're still waiting for redemption in certain areas, pray for patience and trust.

Prayer

Father, thank You for Your promise to work all things together for good. I trust You to redeem my pain and bring beauty from my brokenness. Help me to see Your hand at work and to trust in Your perfect timing. Amen.

June 13

Healing Through God's Word

"He sent out His word and healed them; He rescued them from the grave."
Psalm 107:20

God's Word is a powerful source of healing for your heart. Psalm 107:20 reminds you that His Word has the ability to heal and rescue you from the deepest pits of despair.

The Bible is not just a book of rules or stories; it is a living and active source of truth and encouragement. As you immerse yourself in Scripture, you allow God to speak directly to your pain, offering comfort and guidance.

By meditating on verses that remind you of His love and faithfulness, you can begin to replace the lies of hurt with the truth of His promises. God's Word becomes a balm for your wounds, bringing peace to your spirit and hope to your heart.

- Choose a Scripture passage that resonates with your current struggles and commit to meditating on it daily. Write it on a note card or save it on your phone as a reminder of God's healing power.

Prayer

Lord, thank You for the gift of Your Word, which brings healing and hope to my heart. Help me to turn to Scripture when I feel overwhelmed by pain and to trust in the promises You have given me. Amen.

June 14

Walking Forward in Freedom

"It is for freedom that Christ has set us free. Stand firm, then, and do not let yourselves be burdened again by a yoke of slavery."

Galatians 5:1

When Christ sets you free, you are free indeed. Galatians 5:1 reminds you that His freedom extends to every area of your life, including the pain of your past. You no longer have to carry the weight of old wounds because His love has made a way for healing and restoration.

Walking in freedom requires daily surrender to God. It means choosing to let go of bitterness, fear, and shame, and embracing the abundant life He has for you. Freedom is not just the absence of pain but the presence of God's peace and joy in your life.

As you move forward, remember that healing is a journey. There may be moments of struggle, but God's grace is sufficient to carry you through. Stand firm in the freedom He has given you, and trust Him to guide you every step of the way.

- Reflect on the steps you've taken toward healing and thank God for His faithfulness. Write down three ways you can actively walk in freedom this week, such as extending kindness to someone, practicing gratitude, or embracing a new opportunity.

Prayer

Lord, thank You for setting me free from the burdens of my past. Help me to walk forward in the freedom You have given me, trusting in Your grace and love. Give me the strength to stand firm and the courage to embrace the new life You've prepared for me. Amen.

23

The Power of Forgiveness

J une 15

Forgiveness as a Command

"Be kind and compassionate to one another, forgiving each other, just as in Christ God forgave you."
Ephesians 4:32

Forgiveness is not optional for believers—it is a command. Ephesians 4:32 emphasizes the need for forgiveness, modeled after Christ's own act of forgiving you. Forgiveness reflects God's character and demonstrates His grace through your life.

Choosing to forgive doesn't mean excusing wrongdoing or forgetting the pain it caused. It means letting go of the resentment and bitterness that can poison your heart. Christ's forgiveness is the foundation of your ability to forgive others, no matter how deep the hurt.

When you forgive, you release the weight of anger and allow God to work healing in your heart. Forgiveness brings freedom—not only for the person being forgiven but also for you. It opens the door for reconciliation and restoration in your relationships.

- Identify someone you may be harboring resentment toward. Pray for the strength to forgive them, even if it feels difficult. Reflect on how Christ has forgiven you and let that inspire your decision to forgive.

Prayer

Lord, thank You for forgiving me through Christ. Help me to extend that same forgiveness to others. Teach me to let go of resentment and trust You to bring healing and restoration. Amen.

June 16

The Cost of Unforgiveness

"But if you do not forgive others their sins, your Father will not forgive your sins."

Matthew 6:15

Unforgiveness is costly. Matthew 6:15 is a sobering reminder that holding onto bitterness can hinder your relationship with God. Unforgiveness keeps you trapped in a cycle of anger, pain, and spiritual stagnation.

When you refuse to forgive, you allow the offense to have ongoing power over you. It prevents you from experiencing the fullness of God's grace and peace. God calls you to forgive not for the benefit of the offender but for your own freedom and spiritual health.

Forgiveness doesn't erase the pain or the consequences of the offense, but it shifts the burden to God. By forgiving, you declare that you trust Him to handle the situation with justice and mercy.

- Take an honest inventory of your heart. Are there grudges or unresolved conflicts that weigh you down? Write them down, pray for release, and ask God for the courage to forgive.

Prayer

Father, help me to see the cost of unforgiveness in my life. Teach me to release bitterness and trust You to bring justice and healing. Free me from the chains of resentment so I can experience the fullness of Your grace. Amen.

June 17
Forgiving Yourself

"Therefore, there is now no condemnation for those who are in Christ Jesus."
Romans 8:1

Sometimes the hardest person to forgive is yourself. Romans 8:1 reminds you that in Christ, there is no condemnation. If God has forgiven you, why hold onto guilt and shame?

Self-forgiveness requires accepting God's forgiveness and letting go of the self-punishment you may feel you deserve. Clinging to guilt undermines the power of Christ's sacrifice, which paid for every sin.

When you forgive yourself, you acknowledge God's grace and allow Him to transform your heart. Self-forgiveness doesn't mean ignoring your mistakes but learning from them and moving forward with God's help.

- Write a letter to yourself, acknowledging past mistakes and accepting God's forgiveness. Commit to walking in freedom instead of dwelling on guilt.

Prayer
Lord, thank You for forgiving me through Christ. Help me to forgive myself and to let go of the guilt that holds me back. Teach me to walk in the freedom of Your grace. Amen.

June 18
Forgiveness Brings Freedom

"It is for freedom that Christ has set us free. Stand firm, then, and do not let yourselves be burdened again by a yoke of slavery."
Galatians 5:1

Forgiveness is a path to freedom. When you choose to forgive, you break free from the chains of anger, resentment, and bitterness. Galatians 5:1 reminds you that Christ's desire is for you to live in freedom, unburdened by the weight of unforgiveness.

Holding onto a grudge can feel like control, but it actually enslaves you to the pain of the past. Forgiveness releases that burden and allows you to experience God's peace and joy.

Freedom through forgiveness doesn't mean forgetting the hurt. It means choosing not to let it define or control you anymore. Trust God to bring healing and restoration as you walk forward in faith.

- Reflect on an area where unforgiveness has been holding you back. Pray for God's strength to release it and embrace the freedom He offers through forgiveness.

Prayer

Lord, thank You for the freedom You give through forgiveness. Help me to release the burdens of anger and resentment and to trust You with the healing process. Amen.

June 19

Forgiveness and Reconciliation

"If it is possible, as far as it depends on you, live at peace with everyone."
Romans 12:18

Forgiveness and reconciliation are closely related, but they are not the same. Forgiveness is a personal decision to release bitterness, while reconciliation requires the willingness and cooperation of both parties. Romans 12:18 encourages you to pursue peace wherever possible, but it acknowledges that reconciliation isn't always achievable.

Forgiveness prepares your heart for reconciliation by removing the barriers of anger and resentment. However, reconciliation may require time, trust, and effort from both sides. In some cases, safety or circumstances may make reconciliation unwise, but forgiveness is still essential for your peace.

By forgiving, you open the door for God to work in the relationship. Reconciliation may or may not follow, but the act of forgiving honors God and sets you free. Trust Him to guide you in navigating each unique situation.

- Identify a broken relationship in your life. Pray for wisdom to know whether reconciliation is possible and take a small step toward peace, such as reaching out or offering an apology if needed.

Prayer

Lord, thank You for calling me to live at peace with others. Help me to forgive freely and to pursue reconciliation when it is safe and wise. Guide my steps and give me Your wisdom in mending broken relationships. Amen.

June 20

God's Forgiveness as an Example

"As far as the east is from the west, so far has He removed our transgressions from us."

Psalm 103:12

God's forgiveness is the ultimate example of grace and mercy. Psalm 103:12 paints a picture of His limitless forgiveness, removing your sins as far as the east is from the west. If God forgives so completely, how can you withhold forgiveness from others?

When you reflect on God's forgiveness, it humbles and challenges you to extend the same grace to those who have hurt you. His forgiveness is not conditional or partial—it is total and transformative.

Remembering the depth of God's love and mercy can inspire you to forgive others, even when it feels difficult. Forgiveness is not about fairness;

it's about reflecting the character of a God who has forgiven you abundantly.

- Meditate on the forgiveness you've received from God. Consider writing down how His forgiveness has transformed your life. Use this reflection to help you forgive others in a similar way.

Prayer

Father, thank You for removing my sins and forgiving me completely. Help me to follow Your example and extend that same grace to others. Transform my heart so I can forgive as freely as You forgive me. Amen.

June 21

Living in Forgiveness Daily

"Bear with each other and forgive one another if any of you has a grievance against someone. Forgive as the Lord forgave you."
Colossians 3:13

Forgiveness is not a one-time event but a daily decision. Colossians 3:13 calls you to bear with others and forgive them just as the Lord has forgiven you. Living in forgiveness requires ongoing humility, grace, and reliance on God's strength.

Daily life offers countless opportunities for offense, from minor irritations to deeper wounds. Choosing forgiveness every day prevents these moments from taking root in your heart as bitterness. Instead, you cultivate a spirit of grace and compassion.

Forgiveness is a lifestyle that reflects Christ's love. As you practice it consistently, you grow in spiritual maturity and experience greater peace. Living in forgiveness doesn't mean ignoring wrongs but trusting God to handle them as you focus on His calling for your life.

- Make forgiveness part of your daily prayers. Each evening, reflect on the day and ask God to help you forgive anyone who may have hurt or offended you, even in small ways.

Prayer

Lord, thank You for forgiving me every day. Teach me to live in forgiveness daily, releasing offenses and trusting You with my heart. Fill me with grace and compassion so I can reflect Your love to others. Amen.

24

Healing from the Wounds of Comparison

J une 22

The Trap of Comparison
"Each one should test their own actions. Then they can take pride in themselves alone, without comparing themselves to someone else."
Galatians 6:4

Comparison is a trap that robs you of joy, peace, and contentment. Galatians 6:4 reminds you to focus on your own journey rather than measuring yourself against others. God has a unique plan for your life, and comparison distracts you from that purpose.

When you compare, you either feel inferior or superior. Both perspectives are harmful. Feeling inferior can lead to self-doubt and envy, while superiority fosters pride and judgment. Neither honors God or reflects His love.

Instead of comparing yourself to others, focus on the unique gifts and calling God has placed in your life. Celebrate the successes of others without losing sight of your own blessings. By doing so, you can walk confidently in the path God has set before you.

- Identify one area of your life where you've been comparing yourself to

174

others. Pray for God's help to release these thoughts and focus on His plan for you. Write down three things you're grateful for in your life.

Prayer

Lord, help me to let go of comparison and focus on the unique purpose You have for me. Teach me to celebrate others without feeling less-than. Fill my heart with gratitude for the blessings You've given me. Amen.

June 23

Your Worth Comes from God

"I praise You because I am fearfully and wonderfully made; Your works are wonderful, I know that full well."
Psalm 139:14

Your worth is not determined by how you measure up to others. Psalm 139:14 reminds you that you are fearfully and wonderfully made by a God who sees you as His masterpiece.

The world often places value on appearances, achievements, and possessions, but God's standard is different. He sees your heart and loves you unconditionally. When you base your worth on God's view of you, you can live with confidence and peace, free from the pressure to compare yourself to others.

Healing from the wounds of comparison begins by embracing your identity as a child of God. You are valuable because He created you with care and intention. Let His truth guide how you see yourself, rather than the fleeting standards of the world.

- Spend time meditating on Psalm 139:14. Write it down and place it somewhere you'll see it daily. Reflect on how God sees you, and practice affirming your worth in Him.

Prayer

Lord, thank You for creating me with love and intention. Help me to see myself through Your eyes and to rest in the truth of my worth in You. Teach me to reject the lies of comparison and embrace my identity as Your child. Amen.

June 24

Embracing Your Unique Calling

"For we are God's handiwork, created in Christ Jesus to do good works, which God prepared in advance for us to do."
Ephesians 2:10

God has crafted a unique purpose for your life. Ephesians 2:10 reminds you that you are His handiwork, created for good works that only you can fulfill. Comparing your path to others distracts you from the specific calling God has given you.

No two journeys are the same, and that's by design. God has equipped you with unique talents, experiences, and opportunities to fulfill His purpose. When you focus on your calling instead of comparing it to others, you can fully embrace the life He has for you.

Trust that God's plans for you are good, even when they differ from what others are experiencing. He knows what's best for you and is guiding you every step of the way.

- Take time to reflect on your unique gifts and passions. Write down how you can use them to glorify God and serve others. Commit to focusing on your own journey rather than comparing it to others.

Prayer

Father, thank You for creating me with a unique purpose. Help me to embrace the calling You have placed on my life and to trust in Your perfect plan. Teach me to celebrate the journeys of others while staying focused on my own. Amen.

June 25

Finding Contentment in God

"But godliness with contentment is great gain."

1 Timothy 6:6

Contentment is the antidote to comparison. When you rest in the truth that God is enough and His provision for you is sufficient, you can let go of the desire to measure your life against others. 1 Timothy 6:6 teaches that godliness combined with contentment leads to true fulfillment.

Comparison often stems from the belief that you lack something. Whether it's possessions, achievements, or relationships, the enemy uses this lie to create dissatisfaction. But when you trust in God's plan and His timing, you can experience peace in every circumstance.

Contentment is not complacency; it's a deep assurance that God is your source and provider. By shifting your focus from what you lack to what you have in Christ, you can break free from the wounds of comparison and embrace the joy of God's blessings.

- Start a gratitude journal and write down three things you're thankful for each day. Reflect on how God has provided for you in ways that meet your true needs. Pray for a heart that finds satisfaction in Him alone.

Prayer

Lord, help me to find contentment in You and not in the things of this world. Teach me to trust Your provision and to focus on the blessings You've placed in my life. Fill my heart with peace and gratitude as I rest in Your care. Amen.

June 26

Letting Go of Envy

"A heart at peace gives life to the body, but envy rots the bones."

Proverbs 14:30

Envy is a destructive force that can damage your heart and your relationships. Proverbs 14:30 warns that envy rots the bones, illustrating the spiritual, emotional, and even physical toll it can take.

When you envy others, you focus on what they have and lose sight of the blessings in your own life. Envy also distorts your perception of God, making it seem as though He's withholding good things from you. But God's plans for each person are unique and tailored for their good.

Letting go of envy requires surrendering your desires to God and trusting Him to meet your needs. When you choose to celebrate others instead of envying them, you open your heart to peace and joy.

- Think of someone you've envied and commit to praying for their success and well-being. As you practice celebrating their blessings, ask God to replace envy with gratitude for your own life.

Prayer

Father, forgive me for the envy I've held in my heart. Teach me to celebrate others' blessings and to trust that You have good things in store for me as well. Fill me with peace and contentment as I surrender my desires to You. Amen.

June 27

Renewing Your Mind

"Do not conform to the pattern of this world, but be transformed by the renewing of your mind."

Romans 12:2

The world constantly feeds you messages that fuel comparison, urging you to measure your worth by appearances, possessions, or achievements. Romans 12:2 challenges you to reject these patterns and allow God to renew your mind with His truth.

Renewing your mind involves replacing thoughts of inadequacy and envy with the promises of God's Word. It means focusing on who He says you are rather than the fleeting standards of the world. This transformation requires daily effort and intentionality but leads to lasting peace and confidence in Christ.

By renewing your mind, you can break free from the cycle of comparison and live fully in God's purpose for your life. Let His truth shape your thoughts, attitudes, and actions, drawing you closer to Him.

- Choose a scripture that speaks to your identity in Christ and memorize it. Repeat it to yourself whenever you're tempted to compare your life to someone else's. Let God's Word reshape your perspective.

Prayer

Lord, transform my mind with Your truth. Help me to reject the lies of the world and to embrace my identity in You. Renew my thoughts so I can live in freedom and confidence, trusting in Your perfect plan for my life. Amen.

June 28

Living in Freedom from Comparison

"So if the Son sets you free, you will be free indeed."
John 8:36

Jesus came to set you free—not only from sin but also from the burdens of comparison, envy, and insecurity. John 8:36 declares that when the Son sets you free, you are truly free. This freedom allows you to live confidently in God's love, without being weighed down by the need to measure up to others.

Living in freedom from comparison means embracing your identity as a beloved child of God. It means trusting His plans, celebrating His blessings in your life, and finding joy in the unique purpose He's given you.

As you walk in this freedom, you'll find that comparison loses its power. You'll no longer feel defined by the world's standards but by God's unchanging love. This is the abundant life Christ promised—a life filled with peace, joy, and purpose.

- Reflect on areas where you've experienced freedom from comparison. Celebrate the progress you've made and ask God to continue guiding you. Share your testimony with someone who may be struggling in this area.

Prayer

Father, thank You for the freedom I have in Christ. Help me to live fully in that freedom, free from the chains of comparison. Teach me to trust in Your love and to walk confidently in the purpose You've given me. Amen.

VII

July: Faith in the Waiting Seasons

25

Patience in God's Timing

Trusting God's Perfect Plan

"For I know the plans I have for you," declares the Lord, "plans to prosper you and not to harm you, plans to give you hope and a future."
Jeremiah 29:11

God's timing is often different from ours, yet His plans are always perfect. Jeremiah 29:11 reminds us that God has a plan for our future—a plan filled with hope and good intentions. However, waiting on His timing can be one of life's greatest challenges.

When life doesn't unfold as you expect, it's easy to grow frustrated or anxious. You may wonder why God seems to delay answers to your prayers. In these moments, remember that His perspective is eternal. He sees the bigger picture and knows what is best for you.

Patience in God's timing requires trust. It's not passive waiting, but active faith—believing that God is at work even when you cannot see it. His delays are not denials; they are opportunities to grow in faith, perseverance, and dependence on Him.

- Reflect on an area of your life where you're struggling to wait on God.

Write a prayer of surrender, asking Him to give you patience and trust in His plan. Revisit Jeremiah 29:11 whenever you feel discouraged.

Prayer

Lord, thank You for having a perfect plan for my life. Help me to trust You in the waiting seasons. Teach me to rely on Your timing, knowing that it is always good. Strengthen my faith as I rest in Your promises.

July 2

Learning from Waiting Seasons

"Wait for the Lord; be strong and take heart and wait for the Lord."
Psalm 27:14

Waiting can feel like wasted time, but in God's economy, waiting is never wasted. Psalm 27:14 encourages you to wait on the Lord with strength and courage, trusting that He is working even in the silence.

Waiting seasons are often times of preparation. God uses them to refine your character, build your faith, and draw you closer to Him. Think of the stories of Joseph, David, and others in the Bible who experienced long seasons of waiting before stepping into their God-given purposes. These periods were not delays but essential parts of their journeys.

As you wait, focus on seeking God rather than the outcome. Use this time to grow in prayer, study His Word, and deepen your relationship with Him. Trust that He is preparing you for something far greater than you can imagine.

- Make a list of ways you can actively seek God during your waiting season, such as reading a specific Bible study or dedicating more time to prayer. Commit to focusing on Him rather than the outcome.

Prayer

Lord, teach me to wait with strength and courage. Help me to see waiting as an opportunity to grow closer to You. Prepare my heart for what You have planned, and remind me that Your timing is always perfect. Amen.

July 3

Delighting in God During Delays

"Take delight in the Lord, and He will give you the desires of your heart."
Psalm 37:4

When faced with delays, it's easy to focus on what you lack rather than delighting in the Lord. Psalm 37:4 encourages you to shift your focus from your unmet desires to the One who fulfills them.

Delighting in God means finding your joy and satisfaction in Him above all else. It's about trusting that His presence is enough, even when your prayers seem unanswered. As you delight in Him, your desires begin to align with His will, and you discover a deeper sense of peace and contentment.

Patience in God's timing isn't about enduring with gritted teeth; it's about finding joy in His presence while trusting His plans. When you delight in Him, delays become opportunities to experience His goodness in new ways.

- Spend time in worship and gratitude today. List five things about God's character that bring you joy. Focus on delighting in Him rather than dwelling on your waiting season.

Prayer

Lord, help me to find my delight in You rather than in my circumstances. Teach me to trust Your timing and to find joy in Your presence. Align my desires with Your will as I wait on Your perfect plan. Amen.

July 4

Trusting God's Timing Over Your Own

Scripture: *"There is a time for everything, and a season for every activity under the heavens."* – Ecclesiastes 3:1

Reflection:

Life is a series of seasons, each governed by God's perfect timing. Ecclesiastes 3:1 reminds us that every moment in life serves a purpose, even when it doesn't align with our expectations. Trusting God's timing means surrendering control and embracing the truth that His ways are higher than ours.

When you try to rush ahead of God, you may find frustration and disappointment. But when you trust His timing, you experience peace, even in the waiting. God knows what you need and when you need it. His timing is not about convenience but about aligning everything for His greater purpose.

Patience in God's timing requires faith in His character. He is faithful, loving, and wise. Trusting Him means believing that He is working all things together for good, even when the wait feels long or uncertain.

- Reflect on an area of your life where you've been struggling with impatience. Surrender this situation to God in prayer, asking Him to help you trust His timing. Meditate on Ecclesiastes 3:1 throughout the day.

Prayer

Lord, I surrender my plans and desires to You. Teach me to trust Your timing, knowing that You have a purpose for every season. Help me to rest in Your wisdom and to wait with faith and patience. Amen.

July 5

Resting in God's Sovereignty

"Be still, and know that I am God."
Psalm 46:10

In a fast-paced world, waiting can feel like an inconvenience. But Psalm 46:10 calls you to be still and recognize God's sovereignty over all things.

Resting in God's timing requires stillness—not just physically but spiritually.

When you rest in God's sovereignty, you acknowledge that He is in control. This doesn't mean being passive; it means trusting Him to orchestrate the details of your life while you focus on seeking Him. Resting in God frees you from the anxiety of trying to make things happen on your own.

God's timing often involves teaching us to rely on Him completely. Instead of striving, allow His peace to guard your heart and mind. Trust that He is working behind the scenes, even when you cannot see the outcome.

- Take time today to practice stillness before God. Set aside 10–15 minutes to pray, meditate on Psalm 46:10, and rest in His presence. Let go of any worries and trust Him to work in your life.

Prayer

Lord, help me to be still and trust in Your sovereignty. Teach me to rest in Your presence and to rely on Your timing. Fill my heart with peace as I surrender my worries to You. Amen.

July 6

Persevering in Faith During the Wait

"Let us not become weary in doing good, for at the proper time we will reap a harvest if we do not give up."
Galatians 6:9

Waiting on God often requires perseverance. Galatians 6:9 reminds us that there is a harvest waiting for those who remain faithful. The key is not to give up, even when the wait feels long and discouraging.

Perseverance during the waiting season strengthens your faith and character. It teaches you to trust God's promises, even when you don't see immediate results. Just as a farmer waits patiently for crops to grow, you must trust that God is cultivating something beautiful in your life.

The waiting season is not idle time; it's a time to continue doing good, seeking God, and remaining faithful to His call. Trust that at the proper time, His blessings will unfold, and the wait will have been worth it.

- Identify one good thing you can do while waiting, such as serving others, deepening your prayer life, or pursuing a goal God has placed on your heart. Commit to staying active in faith rather than giving in to discouragement.

Prayer

Lord, give me the strength to persevere in faith during this waiting season. Help me to trust that You are working all things for good. Keep me focused on doing Your will and seeking Your presence as I wait for Your perfect timing. Amen.

July 7

Celebrating God's Faithfulness

"The Lord is not slow in keeping His promise, as some understand slowness. Instead, He is patient with you, not wanting anyone to perish, but everyone to come to repentance."
2 Peter 3:9

God's timing often feels slow to us, but 2 Peter 3:9 reminds us that His delays are not due to neglect but to His patience and faithfulness. He is never late; He is always on time, working according to His perfect plan.

As you reflect on your life, you'll likely see moments when God's timing proved to be better than your own. Celebrating His faithfulness helps you to trust Him more in the waiting. Each answered prayer, every blessing, and even the challenges have shaped you into who you are today.

Patience in God's timing grows when you remember His faithfulness. Celebrate the ways He has worked in your life, and trust that He will continue to fulfill His promises in His perfect time.

- Take time to reflect on God's faithfulness in your life. Write down specific examples of answered prayers or moments when His timing proved better than your own. Use this list to encourage yourself in future waiting seasons.

Prayer

Lord, thank You for Your faithfulness in my life. Help me to trust You in every season and to celebrate the ways You have worked in my past. Strengthen my faith as I wait on Your perfect timing, knowing that Your plans are always good. Amen.

26

Hope When Prayers Seem Unanswered

July 8

God Hears Your Prayers

"This is the confidence we have in approaching God: that if we ask anything according to His will, He hears us."

1 John 5:14

When prayers seem unanswered, it's easy to feel like God isn't listening. However, 1 John 5:14 assures us that God hears every prayer offered in faith. The challenge lies in trusting His will and timing, even when His response isn't what you expected.

Unanswered prayers can feel disheartening, but they are not a sign of God's absence. Instead, they are opportunities to grow in faith and dependence on Him. Sometimes, God's answer is "not yet" because He is preparing something better. Other times, His answer is different from what we envisioned because His plans are higher than ours.

Take comfort in knowing that your prayers never go unnoticed. God is always attentive to the cries of His children. While you wait, trust in His goodness and remain confident that He is working behind the scenes.

• When you feel discouraged by unanswered prayers, write a journal entry listing times in the past when God has answered your prayers or guided you. Let this serve as a reminder of His faithfulness.

Prayer

Father, thank You for hearing my prayers, even when I don't see immediate answers. Help me to trust Your will and timing. Strengthen my faith as I wait on You, knowing that You are always good and faithful. Amen.

July 9

Trusting God's "No"

"My grace is sufficient for you, for my power is made perfect in weakness."
2 Corinthians 12:9

Sometimes God's answer to prayer is "no," and that can be difficult to accept. Like Paul, who asked God to remove the thorn in his flesh, you may wonder why certain prayers seem to go unanswered. Yet in 2 Corinthians 12:9, God reminds us that His grace is sufficient and His power is perfected in our weakness.

A "no" from God is not a rejection but a redirection. It's His way of guiding you toward what is best, even if it doesn't align with your desires. Trusting God's "no" means believing that His plans are better than anything you could imagine.

When prayers seem unanswered, lean into God's grace. Allow Him to strengthen you and trust that He is working for your good, even in the midst of disappointment.

- Reflect on a time when God's "no" led to something better in your life. Write a prayer of gratitude for His guidance and protection, even when His answers were difficult to understand.

Prayer

Lord, thank You for loving me enough to say "no" when it is for my good. Help me to trust Your wisdom and to rely on Your grace in every situation. Teach me to find peace in Your perfect will. Amen.

July 10

God's Delays Are Not Denials

"The Lord is not slow in keeping His promise, as some understand slowness. Instead, He is patient with you, not wanting anyone to perish, but everyone to come to repentance."

2 Peter 3:9

Waiting for God's answers can feel like silence, but 2 Peter 3:9 reminds us that God's delays are not denials. He operates on a timeline that far surpasses our understanding, working all things for His glory and our good.

During seasons of waiting, it's natural to feel impatient or discouraged. Yet God often uses these delays to shape your character, strengthen your faith, and prepare you for what lies ahead. His timing is always intentional, even when it feels slow to us.

As you wait, focus on what God is teaching you in this season. Trust that His promises remain true and that His answers will come in the perfect time.

- Use this waiting season to deepen your relationship with God. Dedicate extra time to prayer, worship, and studying His Word. Focus on growing spiritually rather than dwelling on the delay.

Prayer

Lord, thank You for reminding me that Your timing is perfect. Help me to trust You during the waiting seasons and to believe that Your delays are not denials. Strengthen my faith as I rest in Your promises. Amen.

July 11

The Gift of Persistent Prayer

"Then Jesus told His disciples a parable to show them that they should always pray and not give up."

Luke 18:1

Persistent prayer is a demonstration of faith. In Luke 18:1, Jesus encourages His disciples to keep praying, even when the answer doesn't come immediately. Persistent prayer doesn't change God's mind; it aligns your heart with His will.

When prayers seem unanswered, the temptation is to give up. But persistence shows trust in God's power and faithfulness. It acknowledges that He is your source of strength and that His timing is perfect.

Keep praying, not out of desperation but out of confidence in God's character. Trust that He hears every word and is working behind the scenes for your good and His glory.

- Commit to praying daily for the area in your life where you need God's guidance. Keep a prayer journal to document your prayers and any answers you receive, as a testament to His faithfulness.

Prayer

Father, teach me to pray persistently and faithfully. Help me not to lose heart when answers seem delayed. Strengthen my trust in You and align my heart with Your will. Amen.

July 12

God's Peace in the Waiting

"Do not be anxious about anything, but in every situation, by prayer and petition, with thanksgiving, present your requests to God. And the peace of God, which transcends all understanding, will guard your hearts and your minds in Christ Jesus."

Philippians 4:6–7

Waiting for an answer to prayer can often lead to anxiety, but Philippians 4:6–7 offers a powerful reminder: through prayer and thanksgiving, God's peace becomes your anchor. This peace isn't based on circumstances; it transcends understanding, guarding your heart and mind from doubt and fear.

God's peace is a gift, even when the answers seem distant. Instead of dwelling on the uncertainty, shift your focus to thanksgiving. Gratitude turns your attention to God's faithfulness and His countless blessings. It helps you trust that He is present, working in ways you cannot see.

When you feel anxious about unanswered prayers, remember that God's peace is available to you. It doesn't mean you'll have all the answers right away, but it does mean that you can rest in the assurance of His presence and love.

- Start a gratitude journal. Write down three things you are thankful for each day, even while waiting on God. Use these moments to shift your focus from anxiety to His goodness.

Prayer

Lord, I bring my requests to You with thanksgiving. Fill my heart with Your peace, which surpasses all understanding. Help me to trust You fully, knowing that You are always with me. Amen.

July 13

Trusting God's Perfect Plan

"For I know the plans I have for you," declares the Lord, "plans to prosper you and not to harm you, plans to give you hope and a future."

Jeremiah 29:11

Jeremiah 29:11 reminds you that God's plans for your life are good, even when they don't align with your expectations. While waiting for answers to prayer, it's essential to trust that His plans are not only perfect but also filled with hope and purpose.

Sometimes, unanswered prayers lead to a deeper reliance on God's wisdom. His perspective is eternal, and He sees the full picture of your life. What may feel like a setback to you is often a setup for something greater. Trusting His plan means surrendering your desires and embracing His will with confidence.

God's plans are not always easy to understand, but they are always good. Hold onto this promise as you navigate seasons of waiting, and let it strengthen your hope in His faithfulness.

- Write Jeremiah 29:11 on a note card or save it as your phone background. Read it whenever you feel uncertain or discouraged, reminding yourself of God's good plans for your life.

Prayer

Father, I trust in Your plans for my life. Help me to surrender my will to Yours and to embrace the hope and future You have promised me. Thank You for working all things together for my good. Amen.

July 14

Renewing Your Hope in God

"But those who hope in the Lord will renew their strength. They will soar on wings like eagles; they will run and not grow weary, they will walk and not be faint."

Isaiah 40:31

Isaiah 40:31 is a beautiful reminder that placing your hope in God renews your strength. When prayers seem unanswered, it's easy to feel weary or discouraged. Yet, hope in God is never misplaced. It empowers you to press on, knowing that He is faithful to fulfill His promises.

Renewing your hope means turning your focus from the problem to the Provider. It's a daily choice to trust in His character, His love, and His plan. As you place your hope in Him, you'll find the strength to keep moving forward, even in the midst of uncertainty.

God's timing and answers may not always align with your desires, but they are always perfect. Trust that He is working for your good, and let His hope sustain you as you wait.

- Spend time in worship today, focusing on songs or scriptures that remind you of God's faithfulness. Let this time renew your hope and strengthen your trust in Him.

Prayer

Lord, I place my hope in You, knowing that You are faithful and good. Renew my strength as I wait on Your perfect timing. Help me to trust in Your plans and to rest in Your love. Amen.

27

Strength in the Silent Seasons

J uly 15

God's Presence in Silence
"Be still, and know that I am God."
Psalm 46:10

Silent seasons can feel lonely and disheartening, leaving you questioning if God is present or listening. However, Psalm 46:10 reminds you to pause and recognize God's presence in the stillness. Silence is not absence; it's often an invitation to draw closer to Him.

In the quiet, God refines your heart and deepens your dependence on Him. While His voice may not be as obvious, His presence remains steadfast. Silent seasons teach you to trust Him, not for the answers you seek, but for the assurance of His unfailing love.

Take this time to quiet your spirit and focus on God's promises. Let His Word remind you that He is near, even when you cannot feel Him.

- Spend 10 minutes each day in silent prayer. Use this time to reflect on God's character and promises, asking Him to reveal His presence in the stillness.

Prayer

Lord, teach me to find strength in Your presence during the silent seasons. Help me to trust that You are near, even when I cannot hear You. Draw me closer to You and remind me of Your faithfulness. Amen.

July 16

Faith When God Seems Quiet
"We live by faith, not by sight."
2 Corinthians 5:7

When God seems quiet, it's an opportunity to walk by faith rather than sight. Silence doesn't mean God has abandoned you; instead, it's a chance to grow in trust and dependence on Him.

Faith during silent seasons is an act of surrender, believing that God is working behind the scenes. These times refine your spiritual maturity and strengthen your reliance on His promises rather than your feelings.

When you don't understand what God is doing, cling to what you know: His goodness, His sovereignty, and His love for you. Trust that even in silence, He is shaping you for His purpose.

- Write down three scriptures that affirm God's faithfulness. Memorize them and meditate on them whenever you feel discouraged by His silence.

Prayer

Father, help me to walk by faith when I cannot see or understand Your plan. Strengthen my trust in You and remind me of Your faithfulness. Thank You for working in my life, even when You seem quiet. Amen.

July 17

Growth in the Waiting
"Let perseverance finish its work so that you may be mature and complete, not

lacking anything."
James 1:4

Silent seasons often come with waiting, which can feel frustrating and endless. However, James 1:4 reminds you that perseverance leads to spiritual growth and maturity. God uses these times to shape your character and draw you closer to Him.

In the waiting, God develops qualities such as patience, humility, and trust. These silent seasons may feel unproductive, but they are often where the deepest growth happens. Trust that God is using this time to prepare you for the blessings and challenges ahead.

Instead of focusing on what you're waiting for, focus on who you're becoming through the process.

- Identify one area where you've grown during a past waiting season. Thank God for the growth and ask Him to continue refining you in the current season.

Prayer

Lord, thank You for using silent seasons to grow my faith and shape my character. Help me to persevere with patience and to trust in Your perfect plan. Use this time to make me more like You. Amen.

July 18

God's Timing is Perfect

"He has made everything beautiful in its time."
Ecclesiastes 3:11

God's silence is never wasted; it aligns with His perfect timing. Ecclesiastes 3:11 reminds you that He makes all things beautiful in His time, not ours. His timing is not just about delays; it's about preparation and purpose.

Silent seasons are opportunities to trust that God is orchestrating every detail for your good and His glory. They teach you to surrender your timeline and rest in His sovereign plan.

Though waiting can be difficult, it's a reminder that God's timing is always worth trusting. He sees the bigger picture and knows exactly when to act in your life.

- Take time to reflect on a past experience where God's timing proved to be perfect. Use this reflection to strengthen your trust in His current work.

Prayer

Father, I trust in Your perfect timing. Help me to surrender my impatience and to rest in the knowledge that You are working all things for my good. Teach me to wait with faith and hope. Amen.

July 19

Finding Rest in God

"Come to me, all you who are weary and burdened, and I will give you rest."
Matthew 11:28

Silent seasons can leave you feeling weary and burdened, but Matthew 11:28 is a reminder to bring your struggles to God. He offers rest for your soul, even when answers seem delayed.

God's rest is not about escaping challenges but about finding peace in His presence. In the silence, He invites you to lean on Him, trusting that He will sustain you. Resting in God doesn't mean giving up; it means trusting Him enough to let go of your need to control.

Embrace this silent season as a time to find refreshment in God's love and peace. Let Him renew your strength as you wait on His perfect plan.

- Set aside time this week to rest in God's presence. This could be through prayer, worship, or simply sitting quietly with Him. Allow Him to refresh your spirit.

Prayer

Lord, I come to You with my weariness and burdens. Thank You for offering me rest in Your presence. Help me to trust in Your peace and strength as I wait on You. Amen.

July 20
Trusting God's Process
"Being confident of this, that He who began a good work in you will carry it on to completion until the day of Christ Jesus."
Philippians 1:6

God is always at work in your life, even when the process feels slow or silent. Philippians 1:6 reminds you to be confident that He will complete the good work He has started in you.

Silent seasons are part of His refining process. They teach you patience, deepen your faith, and prepare you for the next chapter of His plan. Trusting God's process means believing that He is not finished with you yet and that every step, even the silent ones, is part of His greater purpose.

- Reflect on one area of your life where you can see God's work. Thank Him for the progress and trust that He is continuing to work in the areas that feel silent.

Prayer

Lord, thank You for the work You are doing in my life. Help me to trust Your process, even when it feels slow or silent. Strengthen my confidence in Your promises and remind me that You are not finished with me. Amen.

July 21

Hope in God's Promises

"Why, my soul, are you downcast? Why so disturbed within me? Put your hope in God, for I will yet praise Him, my Savior and my God."

Psalm 42:11

When silent seasons feel overwhelming, Psalm 42:11 reminds you to put your hope in God. His promises remain true, even when you don't see immediate answers.

Hope in God is not passive; it's an active choice to trust Him in every circumstance. It's declaring His goodness and faithfulness, even in the silence. This hope sustains you, giving you the strength to keep moving forward with confidence in His plan.

As you place your hope in God, let His promises anchor your soul. Trust that He is working all things together for your good, and praise Him for His unwavering love.

- Write down a promise from Scripture that speaks to your current situation. Meditate on it throughout the day, letting it renew your hope in God.

Prayer

Lord, I put my hope in You, knowing that Your promises are true and unchanging. Strengthen my faith during this silent season and help me to praise You in every circumstance. Amen.

28

Trusting God in Delayed Promises

J uly 22

God's Promises Are Sure

"The Lord is not slow in keeping his promise, as some understand slowness. Instead, he is patient with you, not wanting anyone to perish, but everyone to come to repentance."

2 Peter 3:9

Delayed promises can test your faith, leading to questions and doubts. However, 2 Peter 3:9 reminds you that God is not slow but intentional. His delays are not denials; they are purposeful.

When God delays, it is often because He is preparing you, aligning circumstances, or working on the hearts of others involved. What feels like waiting to you is God's patient, meticulous work. Trusting in His promises means trusting in His timing and His faithfulness.

God has never broken a promise, and He won't start now. The delay is an opportunity for you to lean deeper into His presence and trust His perfect plan.

- Write down one promise from Scripture that you are holding onto. Reflect on how God has been faithful to you in the past as you wait for this promise to come to fruition.

Prayer

Lord, thank You for Your faithfulness in all Your promises. Help me to trust Your timing and remember that You are never late. Strengthen my faith as I wait. Amen.

July 23

God's Faithfulness Over Time

"Let us hold unswervingly to the hope we profess, for he who promised is faithful."
Hebrews 10:23

God's faithfulness is the foundation for trusting Him during delayed promises. Hebrews 10:23 encourages you to hold tightly to your hope, not because of your own strength but because of His unchanging character.

Over time, you may feel discouraged or tempted to give up on the promise God has given you. In these moments, look back and remember His past faithfulness. Every fulfilled promise in your life is a testimony of His reliability. Trust that He will remain faithful to His Word, even when you cannot see how.

Delayed promises are not forgotten promises. God is faithful, and His timing is always perfect.

- Spend time journaling about past promises God has fulfilled in your life. Use these memories to strengthen your trust in His current work.

Prayer

Lord, thank You for Your unchanging faithfulness. Help me to hold tightly to the hope I have in You, even when I don't see immediate answers. Remind me of Your goodness and love. Amen.

July 24

Waiting with Patience

"Be still before the Lord and wait patiently for him; do not fret when people succeed in their ways, when they carry out their wicked schemes."

Psalm 37:7

Patience in waiting is one of the hardest spiritual disciplines. Psalm 37:7 encourages you to be still before God, resisting the urge to compare your timeline with others. Trusting God means surrendering your sense of urgency and resting in His sovereignty.

When others seem to achieve what you're still waiting for, it's easy to feel overlooked. However, God's promises for you are unique and personal. He has a plan specifically tailored for your life. Waiting patiently is an act of trust, believing that His timing is not only perfect but also best for you.

Choose to embrace the waiting as a sacred time to grow closer to Him.

- Identify one area where you feel impatient. Commit to praying over it daily, asking God to cultivate patience and trust in your heart.

Prayer

Lord, teach me to wait patiently and to trust in Your perfect timing. Help me to be still before You, surrendering my impatience and placing my hope in Your faithfulness. Amen.

July 25

Finding Purpose in the Waiting

"And we know that in all things God works for the good of those who love him, who have been called according to his purpose.

Romans 8:28

God's delays are never wasted. Romans 8:28 reminds you that He is working all things together for good, even in the waiting. Delayed promises often serve a greater purpose, shaping your character, deepening your faith, and preparing you for what's ahead.

Instead of viewing the waiting as wasted time, ask God what He wants to teach you in this season. It's an opportunity to grow in trust, patience, and reliance on Him. The promise is still on its way, but the process is equally important.

Embrace the waiting as a time of preparation and trust that God is working for your good.

- Ask God to show you one lesson or area of growth He wants to develop in you during this waiting season. Write it down and pray about it daily.

Prayer

Father, thank You for working all things together for my good, even in the waiting. Help me to see the purpose in this season and to trust that You are preparing me for Your promises. Amen.

July 26

Trusting God's Timing

"There is a time for everything, and a season for every activity under the heavens." Ecclesiastes 3:1

Ecclesiastes 3:1 assures you that God has appointed a time for everything in your life. Delayed promises are not forgotten; they are perfectly timed. Trusting God's timing means releasing your schedule and embracing His.

While waiting, it's easy to feel anxious or frustrated. However, God's timing is never late. He sees the bigger picture and knows exactly when to fulfill His promises in a way that will bring the most glory to Him and the most growth to you.

Trusting His timing is an act of faith, acknowledging that His ways are higher and His plans are perfect.

- Reflect on how God's timing has worked out perfectly in a past situation. Use this reflection to trust Him more in your current waiting season.

Prayer

Lord, I trust in Your perfect timing. Help me to surrender my impatience and to rest in the knowledge that You are in control. Teach me to wait with hope and confidence in Your plan. Amen.

July 27

Strength for the Wait

"But those who hope in the Lord will renew their strength. They will soar on wings like eagles; they will run and not grow weary, they will walk and not be faint."

Isaiah 40:31

Waiting on God can be exhausting, but Isaiah 40:31 promises that those who hope in Him will find renewed strength. God sustains you in the waiting, giving you the endurance to press on.

Delays can feel draining, but they are also opportunities to lean on God's strength rather than your own. Trust that He will equip you with the patience and perseverance you need to keep moving forward.

Let His strength carry you through the waiting, knowing that He is faithful to fulfill His promises in His perfect time.

- Spend time in prayer, specifically asking God for strength and endurance as you wait. Lean on Him daily for the energy and patience you need.

Prayer

Lord, renew my strength as I wait on You. Help me to trust in Your promises and to rely on Your power to sustain me. Thank You for being my source of hope and endurance. Amen.

July 28

Praising God in the Waiting

"Rejoice in the Lord always. I will say it again: Rejoice!"
Philippians 4:4

Praising God during delayed promises is an act of faith. Philippians 4:4 calls you to rejoice in the Lord always, regardless of your circumstances. Praise shifts your focus from what you're waiting for to the One who is worthy of your trust.

Worship reminds you of God's faithfulness, goodness, and love. It strengthens your heart and renews your hope. While waiting, choose to praise Him, not for the delay, but for His character and the assurance that He will fulfill His promises.

Praise turns the waiting into a time of worship and trust.

- Create a playlist of worship songs that remind you of God's faithfulness. Spend time praising Him daily, even in the waiting.

Prayer

Lord, I choose to praise You in the waiting. Thank You for Your faithfulness and love. Help me to rejoice in who You are and to trust that Your promises will come to pass. Amen.

VIII

August: Self-Worth and Identity in Christ

29

Seeing Yourself as God Sees You

A^{ugust 1}

You Are Fearfully and Wonderfully Made

"I praise you because I am fearfully and wonderfully made; your works are wonderful, I know that full well."

Psalm 139:14

How often do you look at yourself and feel inadequate? The world is quick to point out flaws, but Psalm 139:14 reminds you that you are fearfully and wonderfully made. God created you intentionally and with great care. You are not an accident or a mistake. Every part of you reflects His artistry.

Seeing yourself as God sees you requires a shift in perspective. Instead of focusing on perceived flaws, focus on the truth of His Word. You are His masterpiece, created with love and purpose. When you embrace this truth, your confidence grows, not in yourself but in the One who made you.

• Spend time reflecting on one unique trait God has given you. Write it down and thank Him for it, acknowledging His intentionality in creating you.

Prayer

Lord, thank You for creating me fearfully and wonderfully. Help me to see myself through Your eyes and embrace the beauty and purpose You've placed within me. Amen.

August 2

Loved Beyond Measure

"See what great love the Father has lavished on us, that we should be called children of God! And that is what we are!"
1 John 3:1

The world often ties your value to accomplishments or appearances, but God's love for you is unconditional. You are His child, loved beyond measure. 1 John 3:1 invites you to marvel at the depth of His love.

When you see yourself as God sees you, you begin to understand that your worth isn't tied to what you do but to who you are in Him. You are His beloved child, and nothing can separate you from His love. Let this truth anchor you when doubts creep in.

- Take a moment to reflect on God's love for you. Write down the ways He has shown His love in your life, and let these reminders affirm your identity in Him.

Prayer

Father, thank You for loving me so deeply and unconditionally. Help me to rest in Your love and to see my worth through Your eyes. Amen.

August 3

Created for a Purpose

"For we are God's handiwork, created in Christ Jesus to do good works, which God prepared in advance for us to do."
Ephesians 2:10

Ephesians 2:10 reminds you that you are God's handiwork, created for a purpose. Seeing yourself as God sees you means recognizing that your life has meaning and value. You were created not just to exist but to fulfill the good works He has prepared for you.

When you doubt your worth, remember that God doesn't make mistakes. He crafted you uniquely, equipping you with gifts and talents to impact the world for His glory. Your life is a testimony of His grace and creativity.

- Spend time identifying one gift or talent God has given you. Ask Him how you can use it to serve others and glorify Him.

Prayer

Lord, thank You for creating me with purpose. Help me to embrace the gifts You've given me and to walk confidently in the good works You've prepared for me. Amen.

August 4

Renewing Your Mind

"Do not conform to the pattern of this world, but be transformed by the renewing of your mind."
Romans 12:2

Seeing yourself as God sees you often requires renewing your mind. The world bombards you with messages about how you should look, act, or be. Romans 12:2 calls you to reject these patterns and align your thoughts with God's truth.

Renewing your mind involves replacing lies with Scripture. When negative thoughts arise, combat them with the truth of who God says you are: loved, chosen, and valuable. This transformation takes time, but with God's help, you can see yourself through His eyes.

- Identify one negative thought you frequently have about yourself. Find a Scripture that counters it and meditate on that verse daily.

Prayer

Lord, renew my mind with Your truth. Help me to reject the lies of the world and to embrace who You say I am. Transform my thoughts and align them with Your Word. Amen.

August 5

Your Identity in Christ

"Therefore, if anyone is in Christ, the new creation has come: The old has gone, the new is here!"
2 Corinthians 5:17

When you accept Christ, your identity changes. You are no longer defined by your past mistakes or failures but by who you are in Him. 2 Corinthians 5:17 declares that you are a new creation.

Seeing yourself as God sees you means embracing your new identity. You are forgiven, redeemed, and set free. The old labels no longer apply. Let this truth empower you to live confidently, knowing you are His.

- Write down three truths about your identity in Christ. Read them daily and let them shape how you see yourself.

Prayer

Lord, thank You for making me a new creation in Christ. Help me to live out my identity in You and to leave behind the labels of the past. Amen.

August 6

Clothed in Righteousness

"I delight greatly in the Lord; my soul rejoices in my God. For he has clothed me with garments of salvation and arrayed me in a robe of his righteousness."

Isaiah 61:10

God has clothed you in righteousness, not because of what you've done but because of His grace. Isaiah 61:10 paints a beautiful picture of your identity in Him.

Seeing yourself as God sees you means understanding that you are covered by His righteousness. When He looks at you, He sees the perfection of Christ. This truth frees you from striving for approval and allows you to rest in His grace.

- Reflect on what it means to be clothed in Christ's righteousness. Thank Him for this gift and commit to living in a way that honors Him.

Prayer

Father, thank You for clothing me in righteousness. Help me to walk in this truth and to live in a way that reflects Your love and grace. Amen.

August 7

Living as God's Masterpiece

"You are altogether beautiful, my darling; there is no flaw in you."
Song of Solomon 4:7

You are God's masterpiece, and Song of Solomon 4:7 reflects His deep love and delight in you. Seeing yourself as He sees you means embracing this truth fully.

You are beautiful, not because of the world's standards but because you were created in His image. You are loved, not because of your performance but because you are His. Let this truth guide how you view yourself and how you live each day.

- Speak words of affirmation over yourself today, rooted in God's truth.

Remind yourself of His love and purpose for your life.

Prayer

Lord, thank You for seeing me as Your beautiful and beloved creation. Help me to live as Your masterpiece, reflecting Your love and grace to the world. Amen.

30

Letting Go of Comparison

August 8

The Danger of Comparison

"Each one should test their own actions. Then they can take pride in themselves alone, without comparing themselves to someone else."

Galatians 6:4

Comparison is a subtle trap that can rob you of joy and contentment. In Galatians 6:4, Paul encourages believers to focus on their own actions and identity, rather than measuring themselves against others.

When you compare your life, gifts, or accomplishments to others, you diminish the unique plan God has for you. This mindset often leads to envy, discouragement, or pride, none of which align with God's desire for your heart. Instead, God calls you to celebrate the blessings and gifts He has uniquely given you, trusting that His plan for your life is good.

Letting go of comparison means choosing gratitude and trusting that God's provision for you is enough. It means shifting your focus from others to Him and walking confidently in your unique calling.

- Identify one area where you struggle with comparison. Surrender it to God in prayer and commit to celebrating the successes of others rather than comparing yourself to them.

Prayer

Lord, help me to let go of comparison. Teach me to find contentment and joy in the unique path You've set before me. Amen.

August 9

God's Unique Plan for You

"For I know the plans I have for you," declares the Lord, "plans to prosper you and not to harm you, plans to give you hope and a future."

Jeremiah 29:11

God has a unique plan for your life, tailored specifically to you. Jeremiah 29:11 is a reminder of His intentionality and care in crafting your journey. When you compare yourself to others, you risk losing sight of the specific purpose God has for you.

Comparison often stems from a belief that you're missing out or that someone else's life is better. But God's plans for you are good and filled with hope. He knows what you need, and He will provide in His perfect timing.

Trusting God's plan requires faith that He is working all things for your good, even when life doesn't look like someone else's. You are on your own path, and it is one designed with love and care by the Creator.

- Spend time reflecting on God's faithfulness in your life. Write down three ways He has guided you uniquely, and thank Him for His plans.

Prayer

Father, thank You for the unique plan You have for my life. Help me to trust Your timing and purpose and to let go of the need to compare myself to others. Amen.

August 10

Celebrating Others' Blessings

"Rejoice with those who rejoice; mourn with those who mourn."
Romans 12:15

Comparison often makes it difficult to celebrate others' blessings. Instead of rejoicing, you may feel envy or resentment. Romans 12:15 calls you to a higher standard: to rejoice with those who rejoice and mourn with those who mourn.

When you celebrate others, you shift your focus from competition to connection. It becomes easier to see God's goodness in their lives without feeling threatened. Remember, their blessings don't diminish your own. God's abundance is limitless, and He has enough goodness for everyone.

Learning to celebrate others is a step toward freedom from comparison. It allows you to live with a heart of gratitude and trust in God's perfect provision.

- Find someone to celebrate today. Compliment or encourage them genuinely, thanking God for their blessings and trusting Him for your own.

Prayer

Lord, help me to celebrate others' blessings with a joyful heart. Free me from comparison and fill me with gratitude for all You've done in my life. Amen.

August 11

Contentment in Christ

"But godliness with contentment is great gain."
1 Timothy 6:6

True contentment comes not from comparing yourself to others but from trusting in Christ. 1 Timothy 6:6 reminds you that godliness paired with contentment is a great treasure.

When you focus on what you lack compared to others, you miss the abundance God has already given you. Contentment grows when you recognize that Christ is enough and His provision is sufficient. Letting go of comparison allows you to experience the peace and satisfaction that comes from a life rooted in Him.

- Make a gratitude list today, focusing on the blessings God has given you. Let this list remind you of His faithfulness and provision.

Prayer

Lord, teach me to find contentment in You alone. Help me to trust that You are enough and that Your provision for my life is perfect. Amen.

August 12

Finding Your Worth in God

"For we are God's masterpiece. He has created us anew in Christ Jesus, so we can do the good things he planned for us long ago." Ephesians 2:10

Your worth is not determined by how you measure up to others but by who you are in Christ. Ephesians 2:10 calls you God's masterpiece, uniquely created for His purposes.

Comparison often blinds you to your value. It shifts your focus from God's truth to worldly standards. But God sees you as His beloved creation, equipped with everything you need to fulfill His plan. Resting in this truth frees you from the pressure of comparison.

- Write Ephesians 2:10 on a card or note and place it somewhere visible. Read it daily to remind yourself of your worth in Christ.

Prayer

Father, thank You for calling me Your masterpiece. Help me to see my worth through Your eyes and to live confidently in Your truth. Amen.

August 13

Trusting God's Timing

"He has made everything beautiful in its time."
Ecclesiastes 3:11

Comparison often stems from impatience with God's timing. You see others achieving milestones and wonder when it will be your turn. Ecclesiastes 3:11 reassures you that God makes everything beautiful in its time.

Letting go of comparison means trusting God's timing for your life. His plans for you are not delayed or forgotten—they are unfolding perfectly according to His will. Trust that He knows what is best for you and that His timing is always right.

- Surrender your timeline to God. Pray for patience and trust as you wait for His plans to unfold.

Prayer

Lord, help me to trust Your timing and to let go of impatience and comparison. I know Your plans for me are good and perfect. Amen.

August 14

Living Free from Comparison

"I have learned the secret of being content in any and every situation."
Philippians 4:12

Paul's words in Philippians 4:12 reveal the secret to living free from comparison: contentment in Christ. No matter your circumstances, you can find peace and satisfaction when your identity is rooted in Him.

Living free from comparison allows you to fully embrace the life God has given you. It frees you to celebrate His blessings in your life and in the lives of others. It also strengthens your relationship with Him, as you trust in His provision and plan.

- Pray for God's help to live free from comparison. Practice gratitude daily, focusing on His goodness and faithfulness.

Prayer

Lord, thank You for teaching me the secret of contentment. Help me to live free from comparison and to find my satisfaction in You alone. Amen.

31

Reclaiming Your Worth in God

August 15

Understanding Your Value

"Are not five sparrows sold for two pennies? Yet not one of them is forgotten by God. Indeed, the very hairs of your head are all numbered. Don't be afraid; you are worth more than many sparrows."

Luke 12:6-7

In a world that measures worth by achievements, appearances, or status, it's easy to lose sight of your value. But God's love for you is not based on worldly standards—it's unconditional and immeasurable.

Jesus reminds us in Luke 12 that we are deeply valued by God, who knows even the smallest details about us, such as the number of hairs on our heads. This is a powerful affirmation that our worth is intrinsic, rooted in being His beloved creation.

Reclaiming your worth means rejecting the lies of the enemy that tell you you're not good enough. It means embracing the truth of God's Word, which declares that you are loved, chosen, and precious in His sight.

- Identify one area where you've doubted your worth. Write a declaration of God's truth about who you are and speak it over yourself daily.

Prayer

Father, thank You for reminding me of my worth in Your eyes. Help me to reject lies and embrace Your truth. Amen.

August 16

Created in His Image

"So God created mankind in His own image, in the image of God He created them; male and female He created them."
Genesis 1:27

From the very beginning, God created you in His image, giving you inherent worth and dignity. Being made in His likeness means you carry His creativity, love, and purpose within you.

When life makes you feel insignificant, remember that you are a reflection of the Creator. This truth sets you apart and elevates your worth beyond anything the world can offer. Embracing this identity can transform how you view yourself and others, allowing you to walk confidently in His purpose for your life.

- Meditate on Genesis 1:27 today. Reflect on how being created in God's image affects your self-perception and how you treat others.

Prayer

Lord, thank You for creating me in Your image. Help me to see myself and others through Your eyes. Amen.

August 17

Worth Rooted in Redemption

"But God demonstrates His own love for us in this: While we were still sinners, Christ died for us."
Romans 5:8

Your worth is not determined by what you do but by what Christ has done for you. Romans 5:8 reveals the depth of God's love: even while you were still a sinner, Jesus gave His life for you. This act of redemption is the ultimate affirmation of your value.

When feelings of unworthiness creep in, look to the cross. It stands as an eternal reminder that you are so deeply loved and cherished that God sacrificed His Son for you. Let this truth sink into your heart and transform how you see yourself.

- Reflect on the cross today. Write a journal entry thanking God for the sacrifice He made to redeem you and affirming your worth in Him.

Prayer

Jesus, thank You for showing me my worth through Your sacrifice. Help me to live confidently in the truth of Your love. Amen.

August 18

Breaking Free from Labels

"Therefore, if anyone is in Christ, the new creation has come: The old has gone, the new is here!"
2 Corinthians 5:17

The world may try to define you by your past mistakes, failures, or shortcomings, but God gives you a new identity in Christ. You are no longer bound by the labels others have placed on you or the ones you've placed on yourself.

2 Corinthians 5:17 declares that in Christ, you are a new creation. This means your worth is no longer tied to what you've done but to who you are in Him. Let go of old labels and embrace the truth of your new identity as a beloved child of God.

- Write down any negative labels you've carried and surrender them to God in prayer. Replace them with affirmations of your identity in Christ.

Prayer

Lord, thank You for making me a new creation. Help me to let go of old labels and embrace my true identity in You. Amen.

August 19

Living as God's Masterpiece

"For we are God's masterpiece. He has created us anew in Christ Jesus, so we can do the good things He planned for us long ago."
Ephesians 2:10

You are not an accident or an afterthought. Ephesians 2:10 declares that you are God's masterpiece, uniquely designed for His purposes. This means you are valuable, intentional, and equipped for the good works He has prepared for you.

Living as God's masterpiece means embracing your uniqueness and trusting that He has a purpose for your life. It means silencing the inner critic and choosing to see yourself as God sees you—worthy and loved.

- Take time today to list three unique qualities or gifts God has given you. Thank Him for how He has uniquely made you.

Prayer

Father, thank You for creating me as Your masterpiece. Help me to see myself through Your eyes and to live boldly in Your purpose for me. Amen.

August 20

Rejecting Worldly Standards

"Do not conform to the pattern of this world, but be transformed by the renewing

of your mind."
Romans 12:2

The world often measures worth by beauty, success, or status, but God's standards are entirely different. Romans 12:2 calls you to reject worldly patterns and to renew your mind with His truth.

True worth is found not in meeting society's expectations but in living according to God's Word. When you align your mind and heart with His truth, you can let go of the pressure to conform and rest in the assurance of your identity in Him.

- Take inventory of any worldly standards you've been trying to meet. Ask God to renew your mind and replace those standards with His truth.

Prayer

Lord, help me to reject worldly standards and to find my worth in Your Word. Transform my mind and heart to align with Your truth. Amen.

August 21

Walking in Worth

"You are altogether beautiful, my darling; there is no flaw in you."
Song of Solomon 4:7

God sees you as beautiful, flawless, and precious. His love for you is not based on performance or appearance but on who you are as His creation. Walking in worth means fully embracing this truth and living in the confidence of His love.

When you reclaim your worth in God, you can walk boldly in His purpose, free from the chains of comparison, self-doubt, or fear. You are His beloved, and that is enough.

- Start each day by declaring this truth: "I am loved, chosen, and worthy in God's eyes." Let it shape how you live and interact with others.

Prayer

Father, thank You for calling me beautiful and flawless in Your eyes. Help me to walk in the confidence of my worth in You. Amen.

32

Breaking Free from Self-Doubt

August 22

Recognizing the Roots of Self-Doubt

"For God has not given us a spirit of fear, but of power and of love and of a sound mind."
2 Timothy 1:7

Self-doubt often stems from fear—fear of failure, rejection, or inadequacy. These fears whisper lies that question your abilities and worth. However, 2 Timothy 1:7 reminds us that fear does not come from God. Instead, He gives you power, love, and a sound mind to face life's challenges.

Breaking free from self-doubt begins with recognizing its source. Is it rooted in past experiences, comparisons, or unrealistic expectations? By identifying the root, you can bring it to God and allow Him to replace fear with His truth.

- Write down a specific area where self-doubt has held you back. Pray over it, asking God to replace fear with His strength and assurance.

Prayer

Lord, help me to recognize the roots of my self-doubt. Replace fear with

Your peace and truth so I can walk confidently in Your purpose. Amen.

August 23

Embracing God's View of You

"I praise You because I am fearfully and wonderfully made; Your works are wonderful, I know that full well."
Psalm 139:14

Self-doubt often clouds how you see yourself, making you forget that you are fearfully and wonderfully made. Psalm 139:14 is a powerful reminder of God's intentional design in creating you. You are not an accident or a mistake; you are His masterpiece.

Embracing God's view of you allows you to silence the inner critic that says you're not good enough. It shifts your focus from your perceived flaws to His perfect workmanship in you.

- Stand in front of a mirror and declare Psalm 139:14 over yourself. Repeat it until you feel it resonate in your heart.

Prayer

Father, thank You for creating me fearfully and wonderfully. Help me to see myself through Your eyes and silence the voice of doubt. Amen.

August 24

Trusting God's Strength in Your Weakness

"But He said to me, 'My grace is sufficient for you, for My power is made perfect in weakness.'"
2 Corinthians 12:9

Self-doubt often arises when you focus on your weaknesses, forgetting that God's power shines through them. Paul reminds us in 2 Corinthians 12:9 that God's grace is sufficient and His power is made perfect in your weaknesses.

Instead of allowing self-doubt to paralyze you, lean into God's strength. Acknowledge your limitations, but trust that He will equip and empower you to do what you cannot do on your own.

- List areas where you feel weak or inadequate. Pray over each one, surrendering them to God and asking Him to show His strength through them.

Prayer

Lord, I surrender my weaknesses to You. Thank You for Your grace and strength that sustain me when I feel inadequate. Amen.

August 25

Overcoming the Lies of Comparison

"Each of you should test your own actions. Then you can take pride in yourself alone, without comparing yourself to someone else."
Galatians 6:4

Comparison fuels self-doubt, convincing you that you're less capable or less valuable than others. Galatians 6:4 encourages you to focus on your own journey instead of measuring yourself against others.

God has given you unique gifts and a specific purpose. Comparing yourself to others diminishes the beauty of your individuality. Breaking free from self-doubt means celebrating who God made you to be and trusting His plan for your life.

- Unfollow social media accounts or avoid environments that lead to unhealthy comparisons. Focus on gratitude for your own blessings and strengths.

Prayer

Father, help me to stop comparing myself to others. Teach me to appreciate my unique gifts and trust in Your plan for me. Amen.

August 26

Speaking Truth Over Yourself

"Death and life are in the power of the tongue, and those who love it will eat its fruit."
Proverbs 18:21

The words you speak to yourself have immense power. Self-doubt often grows when you entertain negative self-talk, but Proverbs 18:21 reminds us that words can bring either life or death.

To break free from self-doubt, intentionally speak God's truth over your life. Affirm who He says you are, even when you don't feel it. Over time, these declarations will reshape your mindset and strengthen your faith.

- Write down five affirmations based on Scripture (e.g., "I am loved," "I am chosen," "I am capable through Christ"). Repeat them daily.

Prayer

Lord, help me to speak life-giving words over myself. Fill my heart with Your truth and renew my mind with Your promises. Amen.

August 27

Taking Bold Steps of Faith

"I can do all things through Him who strengthens me."
Philippians 4:13

Self-doubt often keeps you from stepping out in faith, convincing you that you'll fail or that you're not capable. Philippians 4:13 reminds you that your strength comes from God, not your own abilities.

Breaking free from self-doubt requires action. When you take bold steps of faith, trusting God to guide and sustain you, you'll experience His power working in and through you.

- Identify one area where self-doubt has held you back. Take a small, bold step of faith in that area this week, trusting God to help you.

Prayer

Father, give me the courage to step out in faith and trust in Your strength. Help me to overcome self-doubt and follow Your leading. Amen.

August 28

Living in Confidence

"So do not throw away your confidence; it will be richly rewarded."
Hebrews 10:35

Confidence rooted in God is unshakable because it's based on His promises, not your performance. Hebrews 10:35 encourages you to hold on to your confidence, trusting that God will reward your faith.

Living in confidence doesn't mean you'll never face doubts, but it does mean choosing to trust God more than your fears. As you walk in His truth, you'll find freedom from self-doubt and the strength to fulfill His purposes for your life.

- Begin each day by praying for confidence and choosing one Scripture to meditate on. Let God's Word guide your thoughts and actions.

Prayer

Lord, thank You for the confidence I have in You. Help me to live boldly, trusting in Your promises and plans for my life. Amen.

IX

September: Overcoming Life's Obstacles

33

Persevering in Faith During Trials

September 1

Trusting God's Purpose in Trials

"And we know that in all things God works for the good of those who love Him, who have been called according to His purpose."

Romans 8:28

Trials can feel overwhelming, but Romans 8:28 assures us that God works through all circumstances for good. His purpose is not always immediately visible, but He is weaving every challenge into a greater plan.

Persevering in faith requires trusting that God's perspective is infinitely greater than ours. Like a puzzle piece that seems out of place, trials may not make sense in isolation. But in God's hands, every piece fits into His perfect design.

- Reflect on a past trial where God revealed His purpose. Write it down as a reminder of His faithfulness, and trust He is working similarly in your current challenges.

Prayer

Lord, help me to trust that You are working all things for good. Strengthen my faith when I cannot see Your purpose, and guide me to rest in Your promises. Amen.

September 2

Finding Peace in the Storm

"Peace I leave with you; My peace I give you. I do not give to you as the world gives. Do not let your hearts be troubled and do not be afraid."

John 14:27

Trials often disrupt our sense of peace, leaving us anxious and uncertain. Yet Jesus promises a peace that surpasses human understanding—a peace rooted in His presence, not in the absence of difficulty.

When life feels chaotic, persevere by fixing your eyes on Christ, the anchor in every storm. His peace guards your heart and mind, giving you the strength to endure without fear.

- Spend five minutes in quiet prayer today, asking God to fill your heart with His peace. Focus on releasing your fears and resting in His care.

Prayer

Lord, thank You for the gift of Your peace. Help me to rely on You when trials arise and to trust that You are with me in every storm. Amen.

September 3

The Refining Power of Trials

"These [trials] have come so that the proven genuineness of your faith—of greater worth than gold—may result in praise, glory, and honor when Jesus Christ is revealed."

1 Peter 1:7

Trials test and refine your faith, much like fire purifies gold. Though the process is painful, it reveals what is most valuable: a genuine and enduring trust in God.

When you persevere in faith, your life becomes a testimony of God's sustaining grace. These moments of endurance not only strengthen your relationship with Him but also glorify His name.

- Identify one area where your faith is being tested. Commit to seeking God's presence daily through prayer and Scripture to strengthen your trust in Him.

Prayer

Father, thank You for refining my faith through trials. Help me to embrace this process, trusting that You are shaping me into the person You created me to be. Amen.

September 4
Strength in God's Promises

"The Lord is my strength and my shield; my heart trusts in Him, and He helps me."
Psalm 28:7

Trials often leave us feeling weak and vulnerable, but God's Word provides strength and encouragement. His promises are a shield against doubt and despair, reminding us that He is our help and refuge.

When you rely on God's strength instead of your own, you'll find the endurance to persevere. His faithfulness is unchanging, and His promises are a source of hope in every trial.

- Memorize a Scripture that speaks to God's faithfulness. Recite it whenever you feel weary or discouraged during your trial.

Prayer

Lord, thank You for being my strength and shield. Help me to stand firm on Your promises and trust You fully in every trial. Amen.

September 5

Choosing Faith Over Fear

"When I am afraid, I put my trust in You."
Psalm 56:3

Fear is a natural response to trials, but it doesn't have to control you. Psalm 56:3 reminds us to choose faith over fear by placing our trust in God.

Persevering in faith means shifting your focus from the size of the storm to the greatness of your God. He is bigger than any trial and fully capable of carrying you through.

- When fear arises, pause and pray. Declare your trust in God out loud, reminding yourself of His power and faithfulness.

Prayer

Father, when fear creeps in, help me to turn to You. Strengthen my faith and remind me that You are greater than any trial I face. Amen.

September 6

Leaning on God's Grace

"But He said to me, 'My grace is sufficient for you, for My power is made perfect in weakness.'"
2 Corinthians 12:9

Trials often highlight our limitations, but they also reveal the sufficiency of God's grace. In 2 Corinthians 12:9, Paul reminds us that God's strength is made perfect in our weakness.

Rather than striving to overcome trials on your own, lean on God's grace. His power is more than enough to sustain you and carry you through the hardest seasons.

- Pray daily for God's grace to sustain you in your current trial. Release the pressure to handle everything alone, and trust in His strength.

Prayer

Lord, thank You for Your all-sufficient grace. Help me to rely on Your strength in my weakness and to trust You to see me through every trial. Amen.

September 7
Pressing On with Hope

"Let us not become weary in doing good, for at the proper time we will reap a harvest if we do not give up."
Galatians 6:9

Trials can make you feel weary, tempting you to give up. But Galatians 6:9 encourages perseverance, reminding you that your faithfulness will yield a harvest in God's perfect timing.

Pressing on in hope means believing that God is working, even when you can't see immediate results. Trust that He is using your trials to accomplish His greater purposes, and don't lose heart.

- Set a daily reminder to thank God for His faithfulness, even in the midst of trials. Let this practice renew your hope and strengthen your perseverance.

Prayer

Father, give me the strength to press on with hope. Help me to trust in Your timing and to remain faithful, knowing that You are at work in my life. Amen.

34

Relying on God for Courage

S eptember 8

God is Your Strength

"The Lord is my light and my salvation—whom shall I fear? The Lord is the stronghold of my life—of whom shall I be afraid?"

Psalm 27:1

Life often presents situations that challenge your courage. Fear and uncertainty can arise when faced with difficult decisions, opposition, or unknown outcomes. However, Psalm 27:1 reminds you that God is your strength and salvation.

When you rely on God, you are empowered to face your fears with boldness. His presence as your stronghold assures you that no challenge is too great when He is by your side. Courage grows not from your own ability but from the confidence that God is your protector and guide.

- Identify one area in your life where fear is holding you back. Pray for God's strength to overcome it, and take one small step of faith toward facing that fear today.

Prayer

Lord, You are my strength and my salvation. Help me to rely on You for courage and face my fears with boldness, knowing You are with me. Amen.

September 9

Courage in Obedience

"Have I not commanded you? Be strong and courageous. Do not be afraid; do not be discouraged, for the Lord your God will be with you wherever you go."

Joshua 1:9

Obedience to God often requires courage, especially when it leads you into uncharted territory. Like Joshua stepping into leadership after Moses, you may feel inadequate or fearful about the task ahead.

God's command to Joshua wasn't just an encouragement; it was a reminder of His unwavering presence. When you trust God's promises and walk in obedience, He equips you with the courage needed to fulfill His purpose.

- Write down a specific step of obedience God is calling you to take. Trust Him for the courage to follow through, even if the path feels uncertain.

Prayer

Father, give me the courage to obey Your call, even when it feels challenging. Thank You for Your promise to be with me wherever I go. Amen.

September 10

Overcoming Fear with Love

"There is no fear in love. But perfect love drives out fear."

1 John 4:18

Fear can be paralyzing, but God's love has the power to dispel it. When you understand the depth of His love for you, fear loses its grip because you are secure in His care.

Relying on God for courage means resting in His love and letting it shape your perspective. His love reassures you that He is in control, and you can trust Him completely in every situation.

- Meditate on God's love by reading and reflecting on passages like Psalm 139 or Romans 8:38-39. Let His love fill your heart and replace fear with confidence.

Prayer

Lord, thank You for Your perfect love that casts out fear. Help me to trust in Your love and rely on it for the courage to face each day. Amen.

September 11
Boldness Through the Holy Spirit

"For the Spirit God gave us does not make us timid, but gives us power, love, and self-discipline."
2 Timothy 1:7

God has equipped you with His Holy Spirit, who empowers you with boldness. The Spirit gives you the strength to step out in faith, love others fearlessly, and exercise self-control in difficult circumstances.

Relying on the Holy Spirit means surrendering your fear and trusting Him to work through you. His power enables you to do things you never thought possible, giving you the courage to fulfill God's purposes in your life.

- Pray specifically for the Holy Spirit to give you boldness in an area where you feel timid. Take one step of action, trusting His power within you.

Prayer

Holy Spirit, thank You for empowering me with courage and strength. Help me to rely on You and to act boldly in faith and love. Amen.

September 12

Courage to Stand Firm

"Be on your guard; stand firm in the faith; be courageous; be strong."
1 Corinthians 16:13

Courage is often required to stand firm in your faith, especially in a world that challenges biblical values. Standing firm doesn't mean being confrontational but being unwavering in your trust in God and His truth.

Relying on God for courage means allowing His Word to anchor your beliefs. When challenges arise, you can stand confidently, knowing He is your defender and strength.

- Reflect on a situation where you need to stand firm in your faith. Pray for God's courage to remain steadfast and grounded in His truth.

Prayer

Lord, give me the courage to stand firm in my faith and to trust You in all circumstances. Strengthen me with Your Word and guide my steps. Amen.

September 13

Courage in Weakness

"But He said to me, 'My grace is sufficient for you, for My power is made perfect in weakness.'"
2 Corinthians 12:9

Sometimes, courage means admitting your weaknesses and relying on God's strength. Paul's words in 2 Corinthians remind us that God's grace is sufficient, even when we feel inadequate.

When you lean into God's strength, your weaknesses become an opportunity for His power to shine. This reliance produces courage, knowing that His grace will sustain you through any trial.

- Identify an area where you feel weak or insufficient. Surrender it to God in prayer, trusting Him to work through your limitations.

Prayer

Father, thank You for Your sufficient grace. Help me to rely on Your strength in my weakness and to find courage in Your power. Amen.

September 14

Walking Courageously in Faith

"For we live by faith, not by sight."
2 Corinthians 5:7

Walking in courage requires living by faith, trusting in what you cannot yet see. Faith propels you forward, even when the path ahead is unclear, because you know God is leading you.

Relying on God for courage is a daily decision to trust Him, even when circumstances seem overwhelming. As you step forward in faith, you'll discover that He is faithful to guide and sustain you.

- Take a step of faith today in an area where you've been hesitant. Trust God to provide the courage and guidance you need.

Prayer

Lord, thank You for being my guide as I walk by faith. Help me to rely on You for courage and to trust You in every step I take. Amen.

35

Turning Setbacks into Growth

September 15

Embracing Setbacks as Opportunities

"We know that in all things God works for the good of those who love Him, who have been called according to His purpose."

Romans 8:28

Setbacks can feel discouraging, but Romans 8:28 assures us that God uses all circumstances, even setbacks, for our good. While we may not understand how God works in those moments, we can trust that He is always at work, shaping us for something better.

Setbacks are not the end of the story but an opportunity for God to refine our character, deepen our faith, and strengthen our reliance on Him. When we face setbacks, we have a choice: we can either let them defeat us or allow them to push us toward growth in our walk with God.

- When you encounter a setback, pause and reflect on how God might be using this situation to grow you. Ask Him for wisdom to see the opportunity for growth, even in adversity.

Prayer

Lord, help me to trust that You are working for my good in every setback. Open my eyes to see how You can use this moment to strengthen my faith and bring about growth. Amen.

September 16

Learning Patience in Setbacks

"But the fruit of the Spirit is love, joy, peace, forbearance, kindness, goodness, faithfulness, gentleness and self-control."
Galatians 5:22-23

Patience is often learned in the midst of setbacks. When things don't go as planned, our natural response might be frustration or impatience. But setbacks provide the perfect environment for God to cultivate patience within us.

Galatians 5:22-23 teaches us that patience, or forbearance, is a fruit of the Spirit. It's not something we can manufacture on our own but something God grows in us as we rely on Him. Setbacks test our patience, but they also offer an opportunity to grow in this area, reflecting God's character more deeply.

- When you feel frustrated by a setback, take a moment to breathe and ask God to help you grow in patience. Look for ways to practice patience today, even in small situations.

Prayer

Father, help me to be patient in the midst of setbacks. May Your Spirit grow in me the fruit of forbearance so that I reflect Your patience in all circumstances. Amen.

September 17

Trusting God's Timing

"He has made everything beautiful in its time."

Ecclesiastes 3:11

Setbacks often make us question timing. Why did this happen now? Why didn't things go according to plan? In those moments, Ecclesiastes 3:11 reminds us that God makes everything beautiful in its time. Even in the moments when things feel delayed or out of control, we can trust that God's timing is perfect.

While setbacks can feel discouraging, they are often a part of God's perfect timing, preparing us for what's ahead. Trusting God's timing in the midst of setbacks requires letting go of our desire for control and resting in the assurance that He knows what is best for us.

- If you're feeling frustrated by a delay or setback, practice surrendering your timeline to God. Trust that His timing is perfect, and ask Him for the patience to wait on His perfect plan.

Prayer

Lord, help me to trust Your timing in all things. When setbacks come, remind me that You are in control, and Your plan is always for my good. Amen.

September 18

Finding Strength in Weakness

"But He said to me, 'My grace is sufficient for you, for My power is made perfect in weakness.' Therefore I will boast all the more gladly of my weaknesses, so that the power of Christ may rest upon me."

2 Corinthians 12:9

When setbacks cause us to feel weak, it can be difficult to see any growth. But 2 Corinthians 12:9 reminds us that God's power is made perfect in our weakness. In times of setback, we are often forced to rely on God more deeply, which opens the door for His strength to be made evident in our lives.

Setbacks reveal our limitations, but they also invite us to depend on God in new ways. In our weakness, His grace is sufficient, and His power shines brighter. Embrace setbacks as opportunities to experience God's strength in ways that would not be possible without them.

- When you feel weak or overwhelmed, turn to God in prayer and acknowledge your need for His strength. Allow Him to fill you with His power and grace.

Prayer

Father, thank You that Your grace is sufficient for me. Help me to see my weaknesses as opportunities for Your strength to be made perfect. Empower me to rely on You in all circumstances. Amen.

September 19

Growing Through Adversity

"Consider it pure joy, my brothers and sisters, whenever you face trials of many kinds, because you know that the testing of your faith produces perseverance. Let perseverance finish its work so that you may be mature and complete, not lacking anything."

James 1:2-4

James 1:2-4 teaches us that adversity and trials are not to be avoided, but embraced because they produce growth. Trials test our faith, and through them, perseverance is built. This perseverance leads to spiritual maturity, making us complete in Christ.

Setbacks are an essential part of the growth process. They develop our resilience, deepen our faith, and shape us into the women God created us to be. As difficult as they may be, we can find joy in knowing that adversity has a purpose: to refine us and make us more like Christ.

- The next time you face adversity, remind yourself that it's an opportunity for growth. Ask God to help you persevere and to refine your faith through the trial.

Prayer

Lord, help me to consider it pure joy when I face trials. Teach me to persevere through adversity and to trust that You are growing me into the woman You've created me to be. Amen.

September 20
Shifting Your Perspective

"And we know that in all things God works for the good of those who love Him, who have been called according to His purpose."
Romans 8:28

A setback can sometimes feel like a roadblock, but Romans 8:28 encourages us that in all things, God is working for our good. Shifting your perspective during setbacks is crucial. Instead of seeing them as obstacles, view them as opportunities for God to work in and through you.

God is using every experience, good or bad, to shape your character, strengthen your faith, and lead you closer to His purposes. When you trust His goodness, setbacks become stepping stones to greater things.

- The next time you face a setback, stop and ask God to help you see the bigger picture. Trust that He is at work, even if you can't yet see how it's all going to come together.

Prayer

Father, help me to shift my perspective during setbacks. Teach me to trust that You are working for my good in all circumstances. Thank You for using every part of my journey for Your glory. Amen.

September 21

Moving Forward with Hope

"For I know the plans I have for you, declares the Lord, plans for welfare and not for evil, to give you a future and a hope."
Jeremiah 29:11

Setbacks can sometimes make us feel like we are stuck, but God's plan for our lives is one of hope and a bright future. Jeremiah 29:11 reminds us that God has good plans for us, even when we don't understand the journey.

No matter how many setbacks you face, remember that they are not the end of your story. God is still leading you forward into His purposes, and His plans for you are filled with hope and promise. Perseverance through setbacks positions you to experience God's best for your life.

- When setbacks make you feel hopeless, remind yourself of God's promises. Take steps of faith to move forward, trusting that He is guiding you toward a future filled with hope.

Prayer

Lord, thank You for the hope You give me in every season. Help me to move forward with confidence, trusting that Your plans for me are good. Strengthen my faith to persevere through setbacks and embrace Your purposes for my life. Amen.

36

Victory Through God's Grace

September 22

Living in the Victory of Grace

"But thanks be to God! He gives us the victory through our Lord Jesus Christ."

1 Corinthians 15:57

Victory is not something we earn—it's a gift of grace through Jesus Christ. Many times, we strive to achieve victory in our strength, forgetting that it has already been won for us. 1 Corinthians 15:57 reminds us that God is the giver of victory, and it comes through the work of Christ, not our efforts.

Living in this victory requires us to rest in God's grace, acknowledging that He has conquered sin, fear, and every obstacle that stands against us. When we understand the depth of God's grace, we walk boldly in the victory that is already ours.

- Reflect on areas where you've been striving to achieve victory in your strength. Surrender those areas to God and trust in His grace to carry you through.

Prayer

Lord, thank You for the victory You've given me through Jesus Christ. Help me to stop striving in my strength and rest in the power of Your grace. Amen.

September 23

Grace That Strengthens

"But He said to me, 'My grace is sufficient for you, for my power is made perfect in weakness.'"

2 Corinthians 12:9

In moments of weakness, God's grace becomes our strength. It is in our most vulnerable times that God shows His power, reminding us that His grace is all we need.

Paul's words in 2 Corinthians 12:9 show that victory is not about avoiding weakness but embracing God's strength in it. Grace doesn't just save us; it sustains us and empowers us to overcome challenges. Victory through grace means relying on God's strength to do what we cannot do on our own.

- Whenever you feel weak, speak 2 Corinthians 12:9 over your life. Allow God's grace to strengthen you in those moments and lean into His power.

Prayer

Father, thank You for Your grace that sustains me. In my weakness, let Your strength be perfected. Teach me to rely on You for every victory. Amen.

September 24

Overcoming Through Grace

"For sin shall no longer be your master, because you are not under the law, but

under grace."
Romans 6:14

Grace gives us the power to overcome sin and live victoriously. Romans 6:14 assures us that sin no longer has mastery over us because we are under God's grace, not the law.

This victory through grace doesn't mean we'll never struggle, but it means we are no longer enslaved. God's grace empowers us to resist temptation, grow in righteousness, and walk in freedom. When we rely on grace, we experience true victory, not through our efforts but through the finished work of Christ.

- Identify any areas in your life where you feel stuck in sin or defeat. Bring those areas to God in prayer and ask for His grace to overcome.

Prayer

Lord, thank You for Your grace that frees me from the power of sin. Help me to walk in the freedom and victory that You've given me through Christ. Amen.

September 25

Grace for Daily Battles
"The Lord will fight for you; you need only to be still."
Exodus 14:14

Life often feels like a battle, but Exodus 14:14 reminds us that victory is not about what we can do but about what God does for us. God's grace meets us in every battle, fighting for us and giving us strength.

Through His grace, we can face challenges with confidence, knowing that we're not fighting alone. Victory doesn't depend on our strength or strategy but on God's power and provision. When we are still and trust in Him, we see His grace at work, giving us victory in every situation.

- Whenever you face a challenge, remind yourself to "be still" and trust God to fight for you. Pray for His grace to handle the situation and wait for His direction.

Prayer

Father, thank You for fighting my battles. Help me to rest in Your grace and trust in Your power, knowing that victory comes through You alone. Amen.

September 26

Grace That Redeems Our Failures

"The righteous may fall seven times, but they rise again."
Proverbs 24:16

Failure is not the end of the story when God's grace is involved. Proverbs 24:16 reminds us that though we may fall, God's grace empowers us to rise again.

Victory through grace means that even when we stumble, God is ready to lift us up, restore us, and set us back on the right path. Grace redeems our mistakes and uses them for His glory. With God, failure is never final.

- Reflect on past failures and thank God for how His grace has redeemed those moments. Trust Him to turn your current challenges into victories as well.

Prayer

Lord, thank You for redeeming my failures through Your grace. Help me to rise each time I fall and to trust in Your power to bring victory from my mistakes. Amen.

September 27

Grace That Brings Peace

"The peace of God, which transcends all understanding, will guard your hearts and your minds in Christ Jesus."
Philippians 4:7

Victory through grace doesn't always look like winning every battle; sometimes, it's experiencing peace in the midst of the storm. Philippians 4:7 reminds us that God's peace is a gift of His grace, guarding our hearts and minds even in chaos.

When we rest in God's grace, we find peace that the world cannot give. This peace is a reminder that God is in control, and He is working all things for our good. Victory is not about avoiding struggles but finding His peace in the middle of them.

- When anxiety arises, take a moment to pause and pray, asking God for His peace. Trust in His grace to guard your heart and mind.

Prayer

Father, thank You for the peace that comes through Your grace. Guard my heart and mind in every situation, and help me to trust in Your victory. Amen.

September 21

Living Victoriously by Grace

"I can do all things through Christ who strengthens me."
Philippians 4:13

Living victoriously is not about being self-sufficient but about relying on Christ's strength. Philippians 4:13 reminds us that we can face anything through the power of Christ in us.

God's grace empowers us to live each day victoriously, no matter what challenges we face. This victory is not about perfection but about walking in faith, trusting that God's strength is enough for every situation. Through

His grace, we are more than conquerors.

- Begin each day by affirming Philippians 4:13 over your life. Trust God's grace to strengthen you for whatever the day brings.

Prayer

Lord, thank You for the strength that comes through Your grace. Help me to live victoriously each day, trusting in Your power and not my own. Amen.

X

October: Building Meaningful Connections

37

Godly Friendships and Fellowship

 **ctober 1**

The Value of Godly Friendship

"A friend loves at all times, and a brother is born for a time of adversity."

Proverbs 17:17

Friendship is one of God's greatest gifts. Proverbs 17:17 highlights the beauty of a friend's unconditional love, especially during times of difficulty. A godly friendship reflects the nature of Christ—selfless, patient, and enduring.

In a world where connections often feel fleeting, godly friendships stand apart. They are rooted in shared faith and a mutual desire to grow closer to God. These relationships encourage accountability, provide comfort in trials, and help us celebrate life's victories. Friendships based on God's love not only sustain us in difficult times but also help us become more Christlike.

- Reflect on your friendships and consider how they align with your walk with God. Strengthen those that glorify Him, and seek ways to grow deeper in love and support with your friends.

261

Prayer

Father, thank You for the gift of friendship. Teach me to love my friends as You love me, and help me be a source of encouragement and truth in their lives. Amen.

October 2

The Blessing of Fellowship

"For where two or three gather in my name, there am I with them."
Matthew 18:20

Fellowship is a vital part of the Christian life. Matthew 18:20 reminds us of the power and presence of God when believers come together. Through fellowship, we experience God's love in community, share burdens, and grow in faith.

God created us to thrive in relationships, not isolation. Fellowship helps us stay accountable and strengthens our faith through shared worship, prayer, and encouragement. When we come together in God's name, we build each other up, reminding one another of His promises.

- Make time to connect with your church community or small group this week. Participate in shared worship, prayer, or service projects that strengthen fellowship.

Prayer

Lord, thank You for the gift of fellowship. Help me to seek meaningful connections with others who share my faith, and may our time together glorify You. Amen.

October 3

Building Up One Another

"Therefore encourage one another and build each other up, just as in fact you are doing."

1 Thessalonians 5:11

Encouragement is an essential part of godly friendships and fellowship. In 1 Thessalonians 5:11, we are reminded to actively build each other up in love and faith. Words of encouragement can be a source of strength and hope, especially in times of doubt or struggle.

Godly relationships flourish when we prioritize uplifting one another. By sharing Scripture, offering a listening ear, or simply showing kindness, we reflect Christ's love. True encouragement doesn't flatter but points others back to God's truth and promises.

- Reach out to someone who might need encouragement today. Send them a message, call them, or pray for them, sharing words that uplift and inspire faith.

Prayer

Father, thank You for the opportunity to encourage others. Let my words and actions reflect Your love and bring strength to those around me. Amen.

October 4

Choosing Godly Friends

"Walk with the wise and become wise, for a companion of fools suffers harm."
Proverbs 13:20

The people we surround ourselves with shape who we become. Proverbs 13:20 teaches us that walking with wise, godly friends leads to growth, while ungodly influences can lead us astray.

Godly friendships are not about perfection but about shared values and a commitment to follow Christ. These friends challenge us to grow spiritually, hold us accountable, and inspire us to pursue God's will. Choosing friends who align with our faith helps us stay rooted in God's truth and strengthens our walk with Him.

- Evaluate your friendships. If there are relationships that pull you away from God, prayerfully consider how to set boundaries. Seek out godly friends through church or small groups.

Prayer

Lord, help me to surround myself with friends who inspire me to follow You. Teach me to choose relationships that glorify You and encourage spiritual growth. Amen.

October 5

Forgiveness in Friendships

"Bear with each other and forgive one another if any of you has a grievance against someone. Forgive as the Lord forgave you."
Colossians 3:13

Even the best friendships encounter challenges. Colossians 3:13 reminds us of the importance of forgiveness, modeled after Christ's forgiveness toward us.

Holding onto grudges harms relationships and creates barriers to God's blessings. Forgiveness doesn't excuse wrongdoing but releases bitterness and restores peace. When we extend grace to our friends, we reflect God's love and strengthen the bond between us.

- If you have unresolved conflict with a friend, take steps toward reconciliation. Pray for God's grace to forgive and reach out to restore the relationship.

Prayer

Father, thank You for forgiving me. Help me to extend that same forgiveness to others, especially in my friendships. Teach me to love as You love. Amen.

October 6

Friendship with Jesus

"I no longer call you servants, because a servant does not know his master's business. Instead, I have called you friends."
John 15:15

Our relationship with Jesus is the foundation of all other friendships. In John 15:15, Jesus calls us His friends, inviting us into a personal and intimate relationship with Him.

When we nurture our friendship with Jesus, we become better friends to others. His love teaches us to be patient, kind, and selfless. The closer we draw to Him, the more we reflect His character in our relationships.

- Spend time nurturing your friendship with Jesus through prayer and reading His Word. Let His love guide your interactions with others.

Prayer

Lord, thank You for calling me Your friend. Help me to deepen my relationship with You and reflect Your love in my friendships. Amen.

October 7

Loving Others as Christ

"My command is this: Love each other as I have loved you."
John 15:12

The ultimate goal of friendship and fellowship is to love others as Christ loves us. His love is sacrificial, unconditional, and life-giving. When we love this way, our relationships honor God and serve as a testimony to His grace.

Loving others as Christ loves requires humility, patience, and a willingness to serve. It means putting others' needs before our own and seeking ways to uplift and support them. When we love like Jesus, our friendships and communities become places of healing and growth.

- Look for ways to serve and show love to your friends and community this week. Let your actions reflect Christ's love in practical, meaningful ways.

Prayer

Father, help me to love others as You love me. Teach me to be selfless and compassionate in my friendships and fellowship. May my relationships glorify You. Amen.

38

Encouragement for Mothers and Caregivers

**October 8**

God Sees Your Sacrifices

"And whatever you do, do it heartily, as to the Lord and not to men."
Colossians 3:23

Mothers and caregivers often give so much of themselves, pouring their energy and love into others. Colossians 3:23 reminds us that every act of service, no matter how small or unseen, is ultimately for the Lord. Whether it's preparing meals, comforting a crying child, or caring for an aging parent, your work has eternal value when done in love and faithfulness to God.

It's easy to feel unnoticed or unappreciated, but remember that God sees every sacrifice you make. He values your efforts and delights in your heart of service. Trust that He will provide the strength you need and reward your faithfulness in ways you may not yet see.

- Write down a list of daily tasks you do for others and pray over them, asking God to renew your strength and joy in serving.

Prayer

Lord, thank You for seeing and valuing every effort I make as a caregiver. Help me to serve with love and joy, knowing that my work is for You. Amen.

October 9

Finding Rest in God

"Come to me, all you who are weary and burdened, and I will give you rest."
Matthew 11:28

The demands of caregiving can leave you feeling weary and overwhelmed. Jesus' invitation in Matthew 11:28 is a reminder that He offers true rest for your soul. Resting in Him doesn't always mean escaping your responsibilities but finding peace and renewal through His presence.

God understands the weight you carry. He invites you to bring your burdens to Him, trusting that He will provide strength and refreshment. When you rest in God, you're reminded that you are not alone—He is with you, equipping you for each task.

- Set aside time each day to rest in God's presence through prayer or reading Scripture. Let Him renew your heart and mind.

Prayer

Jesus, I come to You with my burdens. Help me to find rest and renewal in Your presence, knowing that You are my strength. Amen.

October 10

God's Strength in Your Weakness

"My grace is sufficient for you, for my power is made perfect in weakness."
2 Corinthians 12:9

There are moments in caregiving when you may feel like you have nothing left to give. In these times, God's grace sustains you. 2 Corinthians 12:9

reminds us that His power is most evident in our weakness.

When you rely on God, He equips you with the strength you need to continue. Instead of focusing on your limitations, lean into His limitless grace. God's strength is made perfect in you as you trust Him with your challenges, reminding you that you're never carrying the load alone.

- When you feel weak, pause and pray for God's strength. Keep a journal of times when you've experienced His grace in your caregiving journey.

Prayer

Lord, thank You for Your grace that sustains me. In my moments of weakness, let Your strength shine through and guide me in all I do. Amen.

October 13

Love as an Overflow of God's Love

"We love because He first loved us."
1 John 4:19

As a mother or caregiver, your love for others is an expression of the love God has poured into your heart. 1 John 4:19 reminds us that we are only able to love because of the abundant love God has shown us.

Sometimes, caregiving may feel exhausting or thankless. In those moments, let God's love be your source. When you remember how deeply He loves you, it becomes easier to extend that love to others, even when it's difficult. God's love replenishes and renews, enabling you to serve with a joyful and grateful heart.

- Spend time reflecting on God's love for you. Write down ways He has shown His love in your life and let it encourage you to continue loving others.

Prayer

Father, thank You for Your unending love. Help me to love others as You love me, even in difficult moments. Let my actions reflect Your grace and compassion. Amen.

October 12

God's Wisdom for Every Challenge

"If any of you lacks wisdom, you should ask God, who gives generously to all without finding fault, and it will be given to you."

James 1:5

Caregiving often involves making countless decisions, some of which may feel overwhelming. James 1:5 offers reassurance that God provides wisdom when we ask for it. He knows every challenge you face and delights in guiding you through them.

When you seek God's wisdom, He will give you clarity and peace. His guidance is not just for major decisions but for everyday moments as well. Trust that He is with you, equipping you to make choices that honor Him and serve those in your care.

- Before making decisions, take a moment to pray for God's wisdom. Keep a notebook to write down the guidance you sense Him giving and how it impacts your caregiving.

Prayer

Lord, thank You for Your generous wisdom. Help me to seek You in every decision I make and trust Your guidance in all circumstances. Amen.

October 13

Encouragement for the Journey

"Let us not become weary in doing good, for at the proper time we will reap a harvest if we do not give up."

Galatians 6:9

Caregiving can be a long and challenging journey, but Galatians 6:9 encourages us not to grow weary in doing good. Your efforts may not always yield immediate results, but God promises a harvest in due time.

Your work as a caregiver has eternal significance, even when it feels mundane or unnoticed. God sees your faithfulness and will reward your perseverance. Trust that He is working through you to bless and nurture those in your care.

- Remind yourself of God's promises when you feel discouraged. Write Galatians 6:9 on a card and place it somewhere visible to encourage you throughout your day.

Prayer

Father, thank You for Your promise of a harvest. Help me to persevere in caregiving, trusting that my work is meaningful in Your eyes. Amen.

October 14

Trusting God with Your Loved Ones

Scripture: *"Cast all your anxiety on Him because He cares for you."*
1 Peter 5:7

It's natural to feel anxiety about the well-being of those in your care. 1 Peter 5:7 reminds us to cast all our worries on God, trusting that He cares deeply for us and our loved ones.

God loves those you care for even more than you do. When you entrust them to Him, you can rest in His sovereignty and faithfulness. Let go of the weight of trying to control everything and trust that God is working in their lives, even when you can't see it.

- Take time to pray specifically for the people in your care. Release your worries to God and trust Him to provide for their needs.

Prayer

Lord, thank You for caring for me and my loved ones. Help me to trust You fully, knowing that You are in control and will provide for every need. Amen.

39

Finding Community in Christ

October 15

Designed for Community

"And let us consider how we may spur one another on toward love and good deeds, not giving up meeting together, as some are in the habit of doing, but encouraging one another—and all the more as you see the Day approaching."
Hebrews 10:24-25

God created us to live in community. Hebrews 10:24-25 emphasizes the importance of gathering with other believers to encourage, support, and inspire one another in love and good deeds. While faith is deeply personal, it is also meant to be shared and strengthened in the context of relationships.

In a world that often glorifies independence, the Church reminds us of our need for connection. A Christ-centered community provides a place of belonging, accountability, and spiritual growth. Together, believers reflect the love of Christ, shining His light more brightly than any individual could on their own.

- Commit to joining or actively participating in a church or small group. Seek opportunities to serve and encourage others in your community.

Prayer

Lord, thank You for creating me to live in community. Help me to find and nurture relationships that draw me closer to You. Amen.

October 16

The Blessing of Unity

"How good and pleasant it is when God's people live together in unity!"
Psalm 133:1

Unity among believers is both a gift and a calling. Psalm 133:1 celebrates the joy and peace that come when God's people live together in harmony. While differences may exist, the love of Christ binds us together, enabling us to focus on what truly matters.

Unity doesn't mean uniformity. It means valuing one another's unique gifts and perspectives while pursuing the common goal of glorifying God. A unified community reflects God's heart and serves as a powerful testimony to the world.

- Pray for unity in your church and community. Take steps to resolve any conflicts you may have with others, seeking peace and reconciliation.

Prayer

Father, thank You for the blessing of unity among believers. Help me to contribute to harmony in my community, reflecting Your love. Amen.

October 17

Bearing One Another's Burdens

"Carry each other's burdens, and in this way you will fulfill the law of Christ."
Galatians 6:2

Life can be challenging, but God has placed us in community to support one another. Galatians 6:2 reminds us of the privilege and responsibility to bear each other's burdens. This act of love fulfills the law of Christ, demonstrating His compassion and care through us.

When we share our struggles with others, we find encouragement and strength. Likewise, when we help carry someone else's burden, we grow in humility and selflessness. A Christ-centered community thrives when members willingly lift one another up, reflecting the heart of Jesus.

- Reach out to someone who may be struggling and offer your help or a listening ear. Be open to sharing your own burdens with trusted believers.

Prayer

Lord, thank You for the gift of community. Help me to bear the burdens of others with love and compassion, and teach me to trust others with my struggles. Amen.

October 18

Encouragement in Community

"Therefore encourage one another and build each other up, just as in fact you are doing."
1 Thessalonians 5:11

Encouragement is a vital part of a thriving community. 1 Thessalonians 5:11 calls believers to build each other up, fostering an atmosphere of hope and faith. A kind word, a thoughtful prayer, or a listening ear can make a significant difference in someone's life.

In a world filled with negativity, Christ-centered encouragement shines brightly. It reminds others of God's promises and faithfulness, inspiring them to persevere. By encouraging one another, we reflect God's love and strengthen the body of Christ.

- Make a list of people in your community who may need encouragement. Write them a note, send a message, or pray for them specifically.

Prayer

Father, thank You for the power of encouragement. Help me to build others up with my words and actions, pointing them to You. Amen.

October 19

Loving One Another as Christ Loves Us

"A new command I give you: Love one another. As I have loved you, so you must love one another."

John 13:34

Jesus' command to love one another as He loves us sets the standard for relationships in the body of Christ. This love is sacrificial, unconditional, and selfless. It's a love that seeks the good of others, even when it's inconvenient or difficult.

Living out this command requires humility and reliance on the Holy Spirit. It's through Christ's love in us that we can genuinely care for and serve others. A community rooted in this kind of love becomes a powerful witness to the world.

- Look for ways to show Christ's love to someone in your community today. This could be through an act of service, a kind gesture, or simply spending quality time with them.

Prayer

Lord, thank You for Your incredible love for me. Help me to love others as You love me, reflecting Your grace and kindness. Amen.

October 20

Accountability in Christ

"As iron sharpens iron, so one person sharpens another."
Proverbs 27:17

True community includes accountability. Proverbs 27:17 illustrates how believers can sharpen and strengthen one another through honest and loving relationships. Accountability helps us grow spiritually, encouraging us to stay aligned with God's will.

While it may be uncomfortable at times, being open to correction and guidance is vital for spiritual maturity. When done in love, accountability fosters trust, growth, and a deeper connection within the body of Christ.

- Identify a trusted friend or mentor in your community who can hold you accountable in your faith journey. Commit to honest and open communication with them.

Prayer
Father, thank You for placing people in my life to help me grow. Teach me to embrace accountability with humility and grace. Amen.

October 21
Being a Light in Your Community
"You are the light of the world. A town built on a hill cannot be hidden."
Matthew 5:14

God calls His people to be a light in the world, shining His love and truth to those around them. Matthew 5:14 reminds us that our lives should reflect Christ, drawing others closer to Him.

Being a light in your community means living out your faith authentically and lovingly. It's through your actions, words, and attitudes that others can see the hope and joy found in Christ. A Christ-centered community becomes a beacon of light, offering hope and pointing others to the Savior.

- Find ways to serve your community this week, whether through volunteering, encouraging others, or sharing your faith. Let your actions reflect God's love.

Prayer

Lord, thank You for calling me to be a light in the world. Help me to live in a way that draws others to You and glorifies Your name. Amen.

40

Strengthening Your Marriage or Partnerships

O**ctober 22**

Building on a Strong Foundation
"Unless the Lord builds the house, the builders labor in vain."
Psalm 127:1

Strong marriages and partnerships are built on a foundation of faith. Psalm 127:1 reminds us that without God at the center of our relationships, our efforts may lack purpose and lasting success. Inviting God into your marriage or partnership means seeking His guidance, prioritizing prayer, and committing to love as He loves.

When God is at the center, He strengthens your bond, provides wisdom for challenges, and gives you the grace to grow together. A Christ-centered relationship isn't perfect, but it is rooted in eternal truth and sustained by His power.

- Set aside time to pray together daily as a couple. Ask God to guide your relationship and strengthen your connection.

Prayer

Lord, thank You for being the foundation of our relationship. Help us to build our lives together on Your Word and wisdom. Amen.

October 23

Love as Christ Loved

"Husbands, love your wives, just as Christ loved the church and gave himself up for her."
Ephesians 5:25

The love Christ has for His church is the ultimate model for relationships. It is sacrificial, patient, and steadfast. Ephesians 5:25 calls us to embody this same kind of love in our marriages or partnerships, putting the other person's needs above our own and seeking their good.

This love requires humility and a willingness to serve one another. It's not about perfection but about growing together in grace and choosing to love even when it's difficult. With Christ as our example, we can reflect His love in our relationships.

- Think of one selfless act you can do today to show love to your spouse or partner. It could be as simple as a kind word, a thoughtful gesture, or helping with a task they find difficult.

Prayer

Father, teach me to love as You love. Help me to serve and cherish my partner with a heart full of grace and patience. Amen.

October 24

Communication with Grace

"Let your conversation be always full of grace, seasoned with salt, so that you may know how to answer everyone."
Colossians 4:6

Effective communication is essential for healthy relationships. Colossians 4:6 challenges us to let our words be filled with grace and wisdom. This principle is especially important in marriages or partnerships, where open and kind communication fosters trust and understanding.

Words have the power to build up or tear down. When we communicate with grace, we reflect Christ's love and create an environment of safety and encouragement. It's not about avoiding conflict but about addressing it with a heart that seeks resolution and peace.

- Practice active listening during conversations with your partner. Focus on understanding their perspective before responding.

Prayer

Lord, help me to communicate with grace and love. Let my words bring healing and encouragement to my relationship. Amen.

October 25

Forgiveness in Relationships

"Be kind and compassionate to one another, forgiving each other, just as in Christ God forgave you."
Ephesians 4:32

Forgiveness is a cornerstone of any strong relationship. Ephesians 4:32 reminds us to extend the same kindness and forgiveness we have received from Christ. Holding onto bitterness or resentment can create distance, but forgiveness brings healing and restoration.

Forgiveness doesn't mean ignoring wrongs or excusing hurtful behavior. Instead, it's a choice to release the offense and trust God to bring justice and healing. When forgiveness is practiced regularly, it strengthens the bond between partners and keeps the relationship healthy.

- If there's an unresolved conflict in your relationship, pray for the courage to forgive or ask for forgiveness. Take a step toward reconciliation today.

Prayer

Lord, thank You for forgiving me. Help me to extend that same forgiveness to my partner, showing grace and compassion. Amen.

October 26

Serving One Another

"Do nothing out of selfish ambition or vain conceit. Rather, in humility value others above yourselves."

Philippians 2:3

Healthy relationships thrive on mutual service and humility. Philippians 2:3 encourages us to put others' needs above our own, reflecting the humility of Christ. When both partners serve one another selflessly, it creates a relationship built on love and respect.

Serving each other doesn't have to be grand gestures; small, everyday acts of kindness can have a significant impact. Whether it's offering support during a tough day or simply being present, these actions strengthen your bond and reflect Christ's love.

- Identify one way you can serve your partner today, whether it's taking on a chore, offering encouragement, or spending quality time together.

Prayer

Father, teach me to serve with humility and love. Help me to value my partner and reflect Your kindness in our relationship. Amen.

October 27

Facing Challenges Together

"Though one may be overpowered, two can defend themselves. A cord of three strands is not quickly broken."
Ecclesiastes 4:12

Every relationship faces challenges, but Ecclesiastes 4:12 reminds us of the strength found in unity. When you and your partner face trials together, leaning on God as the third strand in your relationship, you become resilient and steadfast.

Trusting God in difficult times strengthens your bond and deepens your reliance on Him. It's not about avoiding struggles but learning to navigate them together with faith and grace. God promises to provide the wisdom and strength you need when you seek Him.

- When facing a challenge, take time to pray together as a couple, asking God for guidance and unity.

Prayer

Lord, thank You for being the foundation of our relationship. Help us to face challenges together, trusting in Your strength and wisdom. Amen.

October 28

Keeping Christ at the Center

"But seek first His kingdom and His righteousness, and all these things will be given to you as well."
Matthew 6:33

The key to a strong marriage or partnership is keeping Christ at the center. Matthew 6:33 reminds us to seek God first in all things, including our relationships. When you prioritize your relationship with God, it naturally strengthens your bond with your partner.

A Christ-centered relationship involves prayer, studying Scripture together, and aligning your goals with His will. It's not about perfection but about consistently choosing to honor God in your actions, decisions, and love for one another.

- Dedicate time each week to pray and study God's Word together. Discuss ways to align your relationship with His purposes.

Prayer

Father, thank You for the gift of this relationship. Help us to seek You first in all we do, keeping You at the center of our lives. Amen.

XI

November: Gratitude and Contentment

41

Giving Thanks in Every Season

November 1

A Heart of Gratitude

*"Give thanks in all circumstances; for this is God's will for you in
Christ Jesus."*
1 Thessalonians 5:18

Gratitude is not about ignoring life's challenges but about choosing to see God's hand in every season. 1 Thessalonians 5:18 reminds us that giving thanks is God's will for us. Gratitude shifts our focus from what we lack to what we have, allowing us to experience joy even in difficult circumstances.

When you practice gratitude, you acknowledge God's sovereignty and goodness, trusting that He is working all things for your good. It's a discipline that helps you grow closer to Him, enabling you to rest in His faithfulness.

- Start a gratitude journal. Each day, write down three things you are thankful for, no matter how small.

Prayer

Lord, help me to develop a heart of gratitude. Teach me to see Your goodness in every circumstance and to give thanks continually. Amen.

November 2

Thankfulness in the Storm

Scripture: *"Give thanks to the Lord, for He is good; His love endures forever."*
Psalm 107:1

Life's storms can make it hard to give thanks, but Psalm 107:1 reminds us of God's unchanging goodness and enduring love. In times of trial, gratitude becomes an act of faith. By thanking God in the midst of difficulty, you declare your trust in His power and provision.

Even when you don't understand why you're facing hardship, you can choose to thank God for His presence, His promises, and the lessons He is teaching you. Gratitude during the storm strengthens your faith and draws you closer to Him.

- During a challenging situation, take a moment to thank God for specific blessings. Focus on His faithfulness rather than the difficulty.

Prayer

Lord, thank You for being my anchor in life's storms. Help me to trust You and give thanks, knowing that You are always good. Amen.

November 3

Gratitude for God's Provision

"And my God will meet all your needs according to the riches of His glory in Christ Jesus."
Philippians 4:19

God is the ultimate provider, meeting our needs in ways we often overlook. Philippians 4:19 assures us of His provision, which goes beyond material needs to include peace, strength, and wisdom.

When we recognize and thank God for His provision, it deepens our relationship with Him and fosters a sense of contentment. Gratitude for what we have shifts our focus from worry to trust, reminding us that God is always faithful to provide.

- Take time today to reflect on how God has provided for you in the past week. Thank Him specifically for His blessings.

Prayer

Father, thank You for meeting my every need. Help me to trust in Your provision and to live with a grateful heart. Amen.

November 4

Cultivating Daily Gratitude

"The Lord has done great things for us, and we are filled with joy."
Psalm 126:3

Gratitude isn't just for special occasions; it's a daily practice that transforms your outlook on life. Psalm 126:3 reminds us to reflect on the great things God has done and be filled with joy.

When you intentionally thank God each day, you become more aware of His blessings. Gratitude nurtures joy and contentment, even in the mundane. By cultivating a thankful heart, you align yourself with God's perspective, finding reasons to rejoice in every season.

- Make it a habit to begin each morning by thanking God for at least three blessings. Let gratitude set the tone for your day.

Prayer

Lord, thank You for the many ways You bless me each day. Help me to cultivate a daily habit of gratitude and to rejoice in Your goodness. Amen.

November 5

Thankfulness in Relationships

"I thank my God every time I remember you."
Philippians 1:3

Relationships are one of God's greatest gifts, yet they are often taken for granted. Philippians 1:3 encourages us to thank God for the people in our lives. Expressing gratitude for others strengthens relationships and reminds us of the ways God works through them to bless us.

When you thank God for the people in your life, it fosters love and appreciation. Gratitude also motivates you to serve and encourage those around you, reflecting God's love in your relationships.

- Reach out to a loved one today and let them know how much you appreciate them. Share a specific way they've been a blessing to you.

Prayer

Father, thank You for the people You've placed in my life. Help me to express gratitude for them and to love them as You do. Amen.

November 6

Thankfulness in Waiting

"Be joyful in hope, patient in affliction, faithful in prayer."
Romans 12:12

Waiting can be a challenging season, but gratitude can transform it into a time of growth. Romans 12:12 encourages us to remain joyful, patient, and prayerful. When you thank God during the waiting, you acknowledge His sovereignty and trust in His perfect timing.

Gratitude in waiting keeps your heart focused on God's promises rather than the uncertainties. It reminds you that He is at work behind the scenes, preparing blessings greater than you can imagine.

- If you're in a season of waiting, write down God's past faithfulness as a reminder of His goodness. Thank Him for what He is doing, even if you can't see it yet.

Prayer

Lord, thank You for working in my life, even in seasons of waiting. Help me to trust Your timing and to remain grateful for Your promises. Amen.

November 7

Gratitude as Worship

"Enter His gates with thanksgiving and His courts with praise; give thanks to Him and praise His name."

Psalm 100:4

Gratitude is a powerful form of worship. Psalm 100:4 calls us to approach God with thanksgiving, acknowledging His greatness and love. When you give thanks, you shift your focus from your circumstances to God's character, glorifying Him for who He is and all He has done.

Gratitude deepens your connection with God, reminding you of His faithfulness and provision. It also renews your perspective, filling your heart with joy and peace.

- Take time today to worship God through thanksgiving. Reflect on His goodness and praise Him for the ways He has worked in your life.

Prayer

Father, I worship You with a grateful heart. Thank You for Your love, faithfulness, and countless blessings. May my life be a reflection of Your goodness. Amen.

42

Finding Joy in Simplicity

November 8

The Beauty of a Simple Life
"Better a little with the fear of the Lord than great wealth with turmoil."
Proverbs 15:16

In a world that glorifies busyness and materialism, simplicity often feels countercultural. Proverbs 15:16 reminds us that a life rooted in reverence for God, even with fewer possessions, is far richer than one filled with turmoil caused by pursuing more.

Simplicity doesn't mean lacking; it means living with contentment and focusing on what truly matters. When we align our hearts with God's priorities, we discover peace and joy that transcends material wealth or worldly success. By letting go of unnecessary distractions, we create space for God to fill our lives with His presence and blessings.

- Take an inventory of your daily life. Identify areas where complexity can be simplified—whether in your schedule, possessions, or commitments—and intentionally focus on what matters most.

Prayer

Lord, help me embrace simplicity and find joy in focusing on what truly matters: my relationship with You and the blessings You provide. Amen.

November 9

Contentment in Christ

"But godliness with contentment is great gain."
1 Timothy 6:6

True contentment doesn't come from external circumstances but from a heart satisfied in Christ. 1 Timothy 6:6 teaches us that pairing godliness with contentment leads to true riches—not the material kind but spiritual fulfillment.

When we rest in God's sufficiency, we stop chasing things that can never truly satisfy. Instead, we recognize the blessings already present in our lives. Contentment simplifies our desires and brings peace, allowing us to experience joy in the ordinary.

- Practice gratitude by listing three non-material blessings God has given you. Reflect on how they bring joy and fulfillment.

Prayer

Father, teach me to be content in You. Help me to find satisfaction in Your presence rather than in the fleeting things of this world. Amen.

November 10

Letting Go of Overcommitment

"Come to Me, all you who are weary and burdened, and I will give you rest."
Matthew 11:28

Our culture often equates busyness with success, but Jesus offers us rest when we come to Him. Overcommitment leads to exhaustion and steals our ability to enjoy life's simple pleasures.

Jesus invites you to lay down your burdens and focus on what He values. By releasing unnecessary commitments, you create space for God's peace and joy. A simpler schedule enables you to be present with loved ones and deepen your relationship with Him.

- Evaluate your commitments. Let go of any activities or responsibilities that don't align with your priorities or God's calling for your life.

Prayer

Lord, help me to release the burden of overcommitment. Teach me to prioritize Your will and to embrace the rest You offer. Amen.

November 11

Joy in the Little Things

"This is the day that the Lord has made; let us rejoice and be glad in it."
Psalm 118:24

Life is filled with small, everyday blessings that we often overlook. Psalm 118:24 reminds us to rejoice in each day as a gift from God. Finding joy in the little things helps us slow down and appreciate His presence in our lives.

Whether it's a warm cup of coffee, a kind word, or the beauty of creation, simple moments can bring profound joy when viewed through a lens of gratitude. Embracing these moments draws us closer to God and reminds us of His goodness.

- Pause throughout your day to notice and thank God for small blessings, such as a smile from a stranger or the sound of birds singing.

Prayer

Father, open my eyes to the simple joys around me. Help me to rejoice in the little things and to live each day with gratitude. Amen.

November 12

Living with Less

"Do not store up for yourselves treasures on earth, where moths and vermin destroy, and where thieves break in and steal."
Matthew 6:19

Modern culture often equates happiness with abundance, but Jesus teaches us to value eternal treasures over earthly ones. Living with less doesn't mean deprivation—it's about releasing the excess that weighs us down and focusing on what truly matters.

When we declutter our lives, both physically and spiritually, we free ourselves to experience the joy of simplicity. Prioritizing God's kingdom over material possessions allows us to live with purpose, peace, and gratitude.

- Declutter one area of your home this week. Donate or discard items you no longer need, and thank God for the freedom that comes with living simply.

Prayer

Lord, help me to let go of material possessions that distract me from You. Teach me to store up treasures in heaven and to live with simplicity and gratitude. Amen.

November 13

Trusting God in Simplicity

"The Lord is my shepherd; I lack nothing."
Psalm 23:1

Living simply requires trust in God's provision. Psalm 23:1 reminds us that with the Lord as our Shepherd, we lack nothing. Trusting Him means believing that He will provide everything we need in His perfect timing.

Simplicity is an act of faith. By letting go of unnecessary complexities, you acknowledge that God is enough. This trust allows you to experience peace and contentment, knowing that your needs are in His capable hands.

- Identify one area of your life where you feel the need for more. Surrender it to God and ask Him to provide what you truly need.

Prayer

Father, thank You for being my Shepherd. Help me to trust in Your provision and to find peace in living simply. Amen.

November 14

The Joy of Simplicity in Christ

"You make known to me the path of life; You will fill me with joy in Your presence."
Psalm 16:11

True simplicity is found in Christ. Psalm 16:11 reminds us that joy comes from God's presence, not from the things of this world. When you center your life on Him, you discover a peace and fulfillment that surpasses anything the world can offer.

Simplicity in Christ means focusing on His will and seeking His guidance daily. It's about letting go of distractions and allowing His presence to fill your life with joy and purpose.

- Spend time in prayer and worship today, focusing solely on God's presence. Let Him guide you in simplifying your heart and mind.

Prayer

Lord, thank You for the joy found in Your presence. Teach me to live simply and to focus on You as the source of true fulfillment. Amen.

43

God's Provision and Faithfulness

November 15
Trusting in God's Provision
"And my God will meet all your needs according to the riches of His glory in Christ Jesus."
Philippians 4:19

The promise of Philippians 4:19 reassures us that God knows our every need and provides for us out of His infinite abundance. Yet, it's often difficult to trust when we feel uncertain or overwhelmed. God's provision may not always come in the way we expect, but it is always sufficient.

Throughout Scripture, we see how God provided for His people in miraculous ways. From manna in the wilderness to feeding the multitudes with five loaves and two fish, He demonstrated that His resources are never exhausted. Trusting in God's provision requires surrendering our fears and believing that He will sustain us in every circumstance.

- Write down a list of your current needs, whether physical, emotional, or spiritual. Surrender them to God in prayer, trusting in His perfect provision.

Prayer

Heavenly Father, thank You for Your faithful provision. Help me to trust that You will meet all my needs according to Your perfect will. Amen.

November 16

Remembering God's Faithfulness

"The Lord has done great things for us, and we are filled with joy."
Psalm 126:3

Reflecting on God's past faithfulness strengthens our faith for the future. Psalm 126:3 reminds us to celebrate and find joy in what the Lord has done for us. When life feels uncertain, remembering His faithfulness gives us hope and confidence that He will continue to provide.

God has been faithful from the beginning of time, keeping His promises to Abraham, Moses, and countless others. His faithfulness extends to you today, ensuring that His plans for your life will prevail. Recalling His blessings helps us cultivate gratitude and deepens our trust in His unfailing love.

- Take a moment to journal about a time when God showed His faithfulness in your life. Share this testimony with someone to encourage their faith.

Prayer

Lord, thank You for Your unwavering faithfulness. Help me to remember and rejoice in all the great things You have done for me. Amen.

November 17

God Provides Peace

"Peace I leave with you; My peace I give you. I do not give to you as the world gives. Do not let your hearts be troubled and do not be afraid."
John 14:27

In moments of chaos or worry, we often seek peace from external sources, but Jesus promises a peace that only He can provide. His peace isn't dependent on circumstances but comes from trusting in His sovereignty.

When we focus on God's provision for our peace, we can release our fears and anxieties. His peace reassures us that He is in control, no matter how uncertain life may seem. This peace allows us to rest, even in the face of challenges, knowing that God's faithfulness will sustain us.

- Spend 10 minutes in silent prayer or meditation, focusing on God's promise of peace. Allow His presence to calm your heart and mind.

Prayer

Lord Jesus, thank You for the gift of Your peace. Help me to trust in Your control and to find rest in Your faithful provision. Amen.

November 18

God's Daily Bread

"Give us today our daily bread."
Matthew 6:11

When Jesus taught His disciples to pray for daily bread, He reminded them to rely on God for daily provision. This request teaches us to trust God one day at a time rather than worrying about the future.

God's provision is not just about physical needs but also includes spiritual nourishment. He offers us the strength, wisdom, and grace we need for each day. By seeking Him first, we acknowledge our dependence on His faithfulness and experience the fullness of His care.

- Begin each day by praying for God's provision and guidance. Trust Him to provide everything you need for that day, both physically and spiritually.

Prayer

Father, thank You for meeting my daily needs. Help me to trust in Your provision each day and to rely on Your grace for strength. Amen.

November 19

God's Faithfulness Through Trials

"The Lord is faithful, and He will strengthen you and protect you from the evil one."

2 Thessalonians 3:3

God's faithfulness doesn't mean we won't face trials, but it assures us that He will strengthen and protect us through them. He is our refuge, guiding us and providing what we need to endure difficult times.

When life feels overwhelming, remember that God is your constant source of strength. He will never abandon you or leave you without help. His faithfulness is unshakable, even in the hardest seasons. Trusting Him in trials allows His power to be made perfect in your weakness.

- Identify a current challenge and invite God into it through prayer. Ask for His strength and protection as you navigate the situation.

Prayer

Lord, thank You for Your faithfulness in every trial. Strengthen me and protect me as I trust in You to carry me through. Amen.

November 20

Trusting God to Provide for the Future

"For I know the plans I have for you," declares the Lord, "plans to prosper you and not to harm you, plans to give you hope and a future."

Jeremiah 29:11

Worrying about the future can be overwhelming, but Jeremiah 29:11

reassures us that God has a plan for our lives. His plans are good, filled with hope and promise. Trusting in His provision for the future allows us to live in peace and faith today.

God's faithfulness in the past is a reminder that He will continue to provide. Surrender your future to Him, knowing that His plans are far greater than anything you could imagine.

- Write down your hopes and concerns for the future. Pray over them, asking God to align your desires with His plans and to provide for each need.

Prayer

Father, thank You for the plans You have for my future. Help me to trust in Your perfect timing and provision for what lies ahead. Amen.

November 21

Rejoicing in God's Faithfulness

"Great is Your faithfulness."
Lamentations 3:23

God's faithfulness is a cornerstone of His character. Each day, we are reminded of His mercies, which are new every morning. No matter what we face, we can rejoice in His steadfast love and unwavering provision.

Reflecting on God's faithfulness fills our hearts with gratitude and trust. He has provided for every need, protected us in trials, and guided us with His wisdom. Rejoicing in His faithfulness strengthens our faith and inspires us to live with confidence in His care.

- Spend time praising God for His faithfulness. Share with a friend or loved one how you've experienced His provision in your life.

Prayer

Lord, I rejoice in Your great faithfulness. Thank You for Your steadfast love and provision in my life. Help me to trust You more each day. Amen.

44

Living Contentedly in God's Abundance

November 22

True Contentment in Christ

"I have learned the secret of being content in any and every situation, whether well fed or hungry, whether living in plenty or in want. I can do all this through Him who gives me strength."
Philippians 4:12-13

The apostle Paul speaks about a contentment that isn't dependent on material wealth or circumstances. True contentment comes from recognizing that Christ is our ultimate source of satisfaction and strength.

In today's world, it's easy to compare our lives to others and feel like we lack something. But when we shift our focus from worldly possessions to God's presence in our lives, we discover that His grace is sufficient. Paul reminds us that whether in abundance or in need, we can find peace and joy in Christ.

Contentment is a heart posture that acknowledges God's sovereignty and goodness. Trusting Him to provide all we need frees us from anxiety and cultivates gratitude for His abundant blessings.

• List three things you're grateful for today, focusing on spiritual blessings or intangible gifts like peace and joy. Reflect on how God's presence has brought you contentment in past seasons.

Prayer

Lord, teach me to be content in You alone. Help me to see the riches of Your grace and to live with gratitude, trusting in Your perfect provision. Amen.

November 23

Recognizing God's Abundance

"The earth is the Lord's, and everything in it, the world, and all who live in it."

Psalm 24:1

God is the Creator and Sustainer of all things, and His abundance is evident throughout creation. He provides for the birds of the air and the lilies of the field, reminding us that He will surely care for us as well.

Sometimes we equate abundance with material wealth, but God's abundance encompasses so much more—peace, joy, love, wisdom, and eternal life through Christ. By recognizing His hand in every blessing, we learn to see life through the lens of His provision and grace.

When we trust in God's abundance, we stop striving for what the world deems necessary and rest in the knowledge that He has already given us all we need for life and godliness.

- Spend time in nature or another setting where you can observe God's creation. Reflect on how His abundance is displayed in the world around you and in your life.

Prayer

Father, thank You for the abundance of Your creation and provision. Help me to recognize and trust in Your sufficiency for every need. Amen.

November 24

Gratitude for Every Blessing

"Give thanks in all circumstances; for this is God's will for you in Christ Jesus."
1 Thessalonians 5:18

Gratitude is the foundation of contentment. When we practice giving thanks in all circumstances, we shift our focus from what we lack to the blessings we already have. This perspective helps us to see life as a gift from God and to trust in His ongoing provision.

Gratitude doesn't mean denying hardships but choosing to focus on God's goodness even in the midst of them. It reminds us of His faithfulness and strengthens our faith as we trust in His plans. A grateful heart is a content heart, resting in the abundance of God's love and care.

- Keep a gratitude journal for the week, writing down three specific things you're thankful for each day. Look for small, everyday blessings that might otherwise go unnoticed.

Prayer

Lord, thank You for Your blessings in my life. Teach me to cultivate a heart of gratitude and to trust in Your faithfulness every day. Amen.

November 25

Living Generously from God's Abundance

"You will be enriched in every way so that you can be generous on every occasion, and through us your generosity will result in thanksgiving to God."
2 Corinthians 9:11

God's abundance is not meant to be hoarded but shared. He blesses us so that we can be a blessing to others, reflecting His love and generosity. When we give freely, we experience the joy of participating in His work and the privilege of meeting others' needs.

Living generously doesn't always mean financial giving; it can include offering your time, encouragement, or skills. Trusting in God's provision enables us to give without fear, knowing He will continue to supply all we need.

Generosity flows from a content heart that recognizes God as the ultimate source of every blessing. It glorifies Him and brings thanksgiving to His name.

- Look for an opportunity to give generously this week, whether through your time, resources, or encouragement. Pray about how you can be a blessing to someone in need.

Prayer

Lord, thank You for Your abundant blessings. Help me to live generously, trusting in Your provision and reflecting Your love to those around me. Amen.

November 26
Resting in God's Sufficiency
"The Lord is my shepherd; I lack nothing."
Psalm 23:1

Psalm 23 beautifully illustrates the sufficiency of God's care for His children. As our Shepherd, He leads, provides, protects, and restores. When we trust in Him, we lack nothing, for His presence fulfills every need.

Resting in God's sufficiency means releasing the need to strive for more and embracing the peace that comes from knowing He is enough. It is a daily practice of surrender, trusting that His provision is always timely and perfect.

When we rest in God's sufficiency, we experience a deep sense of peace and contentment, no matter our circumstances.

- Spend time in prayer, asking God to show you areas where you may be striving unnecessarily. Surrender those areas to Him, trusting in His sufficiency.

Prayer

Lord, You are my Shepherd, and I lack nothing. Help me to rest in Your sufficiency and to trust in Your care for every need. Amen.

November 27

The Danger of Discontentment

"Keep your lives free from the love of money and be content with what you have, because God has said, 'Never will I leave you; never will I forsake you.'"

Hebrews 13:5

Discontentment often stems from a desire for more—more money, success, or recognition. Yet, Hebrews 13:5 reminds us that true contentment comes from God's presence, not worldly possessions.

When we focus on what we don't have, we risk losing sight of the blessings already in our lives. Discontentment breeds frustration and distracts us from God's purpose. But by grounding our hearts in His promises, we find freedom from the endless pursuit of "more."

God's presence is the greatest gift we could ever receive. Trusting in His faithfulness leads to a content and joyful heart.

- Identify any areas where discontentment may have taken root in your life. Pray for God's help in shifting your focus to His blessings and presence.

Prayer

Lord, help me to find contentment in Your presence. Free me from the grip of discontentment and remind me that You are enough. Amen.

November 28

Living Abundantly in Christ

"I came that they may have life and have it abundantly."

John 10:10

Jesus came to give us abundant life—a life filled with His love, joy, and peace. This abundance is not about material wealth but a deep, fulfilling relationship with Him.

Living abundantly in Christ means walking in His truth, embracing His grace, and sharing His love with others. It's a life marked by contentment, gratitude, and trust in His provision. When we live in His abundance, we reflect His goodness to the world and experience the fullness of His joy.

- Reflect on what it means to live abundantly in Christ. Ask Him to help you focus on spiritual richness rather than material gain.

Prayer

Jesus, thank You for the abundant life You offer. Help me to live fully in Your love and to reflect Your grace to those around me. Amen.

XII

December: Reflecting on God's Faithfulness

45

Celebrating Christ's Presence in Your Life

December 1

Recognizing Christ's Nearness

"The Lord is near to all who call on Him, to all who call on Him in truth."

Psalm 145:18

It's easy to go through life feeling distant from God, especially when challenges arise. Yet, the truth is that Christ is always near to those who call on Him. His presence is not dependent on our feelings but on His promise to never leave or forsake us.

When we take time to pause and reflect, we begin to see evidence of Christ's nearness in our daily lives. Whether it's a moment of peace in the midst of chaos or the kindness of a friend, these are reminders that He walks with us.

Recognizing Christ's presence allows us to live with greater gratitude and hope. Celebrating His nearness helps us to draw closer to Him and experience the joy of His companionship.

- Take time today to reflect on moments where you've felt God's presence recently. Write them down as a reminder of His faithfulness.

Prayer

Lord, thank You for Your nearness and faithfulness. Help me to recognize and celebrate Your presence in my life each day. Amen.

December 2

Abiding in Christ

"Abide in Me, and I in you. As the branch cannot bear fruit by itself unless it abides in the vine, neither can you unless you abide in Me."

John 15:4

Abiding in Christ is about living in a close and constant relationship with Him. Just as a branch depends on the vine for nourishment and growth, we depend on Christ for spiritual vitality and fruitfulness.

This abiding is not a one-time action but a daily choice to remain connected to Him through prayer, worship, and His Word. It's in this connection that we experience His peace, strength, and guidance.

Celebrating Christ's presence in our lives starts with abiding in Him. As we do so, His love fills our hearts and overflows into every area of our lives.

- Spend 15 minutes in uninterrupted prayer and reflection today, asking God to help you abide more fully in Him.

Prayer

Jesus, teach me to abide in You daily. Help me to rely on Your strength and to celebrate the life and love that come from Your presence. Amen.

December 3

Christ's Presence in the Ordinary

"Whatever you do, work at it with all your heart, as working for the Lord, not for

human masters."
Colossians 3:23

Christ's presence is not limited to church services or quiet devotional times; He is with us in every moment, even in the mundane tasks of daily life. Whether we're folding laundry, commuting to work, or preparing a meal, we can invite Him into those moments and experience His peace and joy.

When we view our ordinary tasks as opportunities to serve and glorify God, we begin to see His presence in every aspect of life. This perspective transforms the mundane into something meaningful and sacred.

Celebrating Christ's presence in the ordinary reminds us that He is always at work in us and through us, even in the smallest details of our lives.

- Choose one ordinary task today and intentionally invite Christ into it. Pray or reflect on His presence as you complete it.

Prayer

Lord, thank You for being present in every moment of my life. Help me to see You in the ordinary and to honor You in all I do. Amen.

December 4

The Joy of His Presence

"You make known to me the path of life; in Your presence there is fullness of joy; at Your right hand are pleasures forevermore."
Psalm 16:11

The presence of Christ is a source of unparalleled joy. While worldly pleasures are fleeting, the joy that comes from knowing and walking with Him is eternal and unshakable.

This joy is not dependent on circumstances but rooted in the assurance of His love, salvation, and promises. When we celebrate His presence, we're reminded of the hope and peace that only He can provide.

Living with the joy of His presence transforms our perspective, giving us strength to face challenges and a heart that overflows with gratitude.

- Take time today to thank God for the joy of His presence. Write down ways His joy has sustained you in difficult times.

Prayer

Lord, thank You for the joy that comes from being in Your presence. Fill my heart with Your peace and remind me of the hope I have in You. Amen.

December 5

Sharing Christ's Presence with Others

"Let your light shine before others, that they may see your good deeds and glorify your Father in heaven."
Matthew 5:16

As followers of Christ, we are called to reflect His presence to those around us. When we live in His love and peace, we naturally become a light to others, pointing them to His grace.

Celebrating Christ's presence includes sharing it with others—through acts of kindness, words of encouragement, and living a life that honors Him. In doing so, we become vessels of His love, bringing hope and light to a world in need.

By staying close to Christ, we're equipped to share His presence authentically and effectively, drawing others closer to Him.

- Look for an opportunity to share Christ's presence with someone today, whether through a kind word, a listening ear, or a small act of service.

Prayer

Lord, thank You for the privilege of reflecting Your presence to others.

Help me to be a light in the world and to share Your love freely. Amen.

December 6

Trusting in His Constant Presence

"And surely I am with you always, to the very end of the age."
Matthew 28:20

One of the most comforting truths of the Christian faith is the promise that Christ is always with us. No matter where we go or what we face, He walks alongside us, offering His guidance, comfort, and strength.

This promise provides the assurance that we are never alone. Even in moments of doubt or fear, we can trust in His unchanging presence. Celebrating this truth helps us to face life's challenges with courage and hope.

Trusting in His constant presence gives us peace, knowing that He is our refuge and strength in every season.

- Reflect on a time when you felt God's presence in a challenging situation. Thank Him for being with you and for His ongoing faithfulness.

Prayer

Lord, thank You for Your constant presence in my life. Help me to trust in Your nearness and to rest in the assurance that I am never alone. Amen.

December 7

Living in Daily Celebration of Christ

"Rejoice in the Lord always. I will say it again: Rejoice!"
Philippians 4:4

Living in daily celebration of Christ's presence means rejoicing in Him regardless of our circumstances. It's a life marked by worship, gratitude, and a deep awareness of His love and grace.

This celebration isn't reserved for special occasions; it's a daily choice to focus on His goodness and to live in the joy of His salvation. By celebrating His presence, we glorify Him and strengthen our faith.

Living in this way transforms our hearts and impacts those around us, pointing them to the hope and joy found in Christ.

- Begin each day this week by praising God for His presence in your life. Let this practice shape your attitude and interactions throughout the day.

Prayer

Jesus, I rejoice in Your presence and celebrate Your love and faithfulness. Help me to live each day with a heart full of gratitude and praise for You. Amen.

46

Preparing Your Heart for Christmas

December 8

The Promise of the Savior

"Therefore the Lord Himself will give you a sign: The virgin will conceive and give birth to a son, and will call Him Immanuel."

Isaiah 7:14

Christmas is a season of celebration, but its significance lies in the fulfillment of God's promise to send a Savior. Long before Jesus was born, God assured His people that redemption was coming. The name "Immanuel," meaning "God with us," captures the heart of Christmas: God's desire to dwell with His people.

As we prepare for Christmas, it's important to reflect on this promise and its fulfillment in Jesus Christ. The busyness of the season can distract us, but pausing to remember the reason for the celebration brings our focus back to God's incredible love.

Let this week be a time to dwell on the miracle of Christ's birth and the hope it brings. Just as God kept His promise to send a Savior, we can trust Him to fulfill His promises in our lives.

• Set aside time today to read the prophecy of Jesus' birth in Isaiah. Reflect

319

on how God's promises are fulfilled in Christ.

Prayer

Lord, thank You for sending Jesus as the fulfillment of Your promises. Help me to prepare my heart for Christmas by focusing on the miracle of His birth. Amen.

December 9

A Heart of Anticipation

"But when the set time had fully come, God sent His Son, born of a woman, born under the law." Galatians 4:4

Christmas is a time of joyful anticipation, much like the Israelites experienced as they awaited the coming Messiah. God's timing was perfect—Jesus came when the world was ready to receive Him.

Today, we continue to live in anticipation—not of Christ's first coming, but of His return. Preparing our hearts for Christmas involves cultivating that same sense of expectancy. Just as the shepherds and wise men looked for signs of His arrival, we too should look for ways God is moving in our lives and world.

As you anticipate Christmas, take time to align your heart with God's purposes. Let the season remind you of the hope and joy that comes from living with eyes fixed on Jesus.

- Spend time reflecting on the ways you see God working in your life. Write down areas where you need to trust His timing.

Prayer

Heavenly Father, teach me to wait with joyful anticipation for Your plans to unfold. Help me prepare my heart for Christmas by focusing on Your perfect timing. Amen.

December 10

Worship as Preparation

"Come, let us bow down in worship, let us kneel before the Lord our Maker."
Psalm 95:6

The shepherds and angels responded to Christ's birth with worship, and so should we. Worship is a powerful way to prepare our hearts for Christmas, as it shifts our focus from ourselves to the wonder of God's gift to humanity.

Worship doesn't only happen in a church setting. It happens in quiet moments of prayer, in songs sung during the day, and in acts of love toward others. By intentionally worshiping Christ during the Christmas season, we open our hearts to the peace and joy He brings.

Take time to reflect on who Jesus is and why His birth is worth celebrating. Worship transforms the Christmas season from a series of tasks into a time of genuine connection with God.

- Create a worship playlist of your favorite Christmas hymns or songs about Jesus' birth. Spend time each day listening and reflecting on the lyrics.

Prayer

Lord, I come before You in worship, honoring the gift of Your Son. May my heart be filled with gratitude and praise this Christmas season. Amen.

December 11

Reflecting Christ's Generosity

"For God so loved the world that He gave His one and only Son, that whoever believes in Him shall not perish but have eternal life."
John 3:16

Christmas is a season of giving, inspired by the greatest gift of all: Jesus Christ. God's gift to us was an act of sacrificial love, given freely for our salvation. As we prepare our hearts for Christmas, reflecting this generosity in our own lives helps us share the love of Christ with others.

Generosity isn't just about material gifts; it's about giving our time, attention, and kindness. When we extend love to others, we mirror the heart of God and point them to the true meaning of Christmas.

Let this season be a time of intentional generosity that reflects Christ's love. In giving, we prepare our hearts to receive the fullness of God's blessings.

- Think of someone in need this Christmas season, and find a way to bless them—whether through a gift, a kind gesture, or spending time with them.

Prayer

Lord, thank You for the gift of Jesus. Teach me to be generous in reflecting Your love to others this Christmas season. Amen.

December 12

Resting in God's Peace

"Glory to God in the highest heaven, and on earth peace to those on whom His favor rests." Luke 2:14

In the hustle and bustle of the Christmas season, it's easy to lose sight of the peace that Jesus came to bring. The angels proclaimed peace on earth at His birth, a peace that transcends circumstances and calms our hearts.

Preparing your heart for Christmas involves finding moments of rest and stillness in God's presence. When we make room for His peace, we're better able to experience the true joy of the season.

Let the peace of Christ guard your heart and mind as you prepare to celebrate His birth. Remember that His peace is a gift, freely given to all who trust in Him.

- Set aside time each day this week to sit quietly in God's presence. Meditate on His peace and let it fill your heart.

Prayer

Prince of Peace, I come to You seeking rest for my soul. Help me to prepare for Christmas by resting in the peace only You can give. Amen.

December 13

Celebrating the Light of the World

"I am the light of the world. Whoever follows Me will never walk in darkness but will have the light of life."

John 8:12

The birth of Jesus brought light into a world darkened by sin. He is the Light of the World, guiding us out of darkness and into the hope of eternal life.

As you prepare your heart for Christmas, celebrate the light of Christ in your life. His light dispels fear, doubt, and despair, replacing them with hope and joy. Let this season remind you of the transformative power of His presence.

By living as children of the light, we reflect His glory and invite others to experience the hope of Christmas.

- Light a candle or string lights in your home as a reminder of Christ's light. Reflect on how His presence has brought hope and clarity to your life.

Prayer

Jesus, thank You for being the Light of the World. Shine Your light in my heart and help me to reflect it to others this Christmas season. Amen.

December 14

Rejoicing in the Gift of Christ

"Today in the town of David a Savior has been born to you; He is the Messiah, the Lord." Luke 2:11

Christmas is a time of great rejoicing because it celebrates the greatest gift humanity has ever received: Jesus Christ. His birth was a declaration of God's love and His plan to redeem the world.

Rejoicing in this gift goes beyond the festivities—it's about letting the joy of salvation fill your heart. This joy is unshakable, rooted in the knowledge that through Jesus, we have eternal hope and a restored relationship with God.

As you prepare for Christmas, take time to thank God for the gift of His Son. Let the joy of Christ's birth overflow in your heart and life.

- End your day by thanking God for specific ways Jesus has impacted your life. Let gratitude shape your celebration of Christmas.

Prayer

Heavenly Father, I rejoice in the gift of Jesus Christ. Thank You for loving me so deeply and for the hope I have in Him. Help me to celebrate this gift with a heart full of gratitude. Amen.

47

A Year-End Reflection: Counting Your Blessings

D**ecember 15**

Remembering God's Faithfulness

"The Lord has done great things for us, and we are filled with joy."
Psalm 126:3

As the year draws to a close, it is important to pause and reflect on God's faithfulness. From the smallest moments of provision to the larger breakthroughs, God has been present every step of the way. Life can often feel overwhelming, and we may forget the blessings that surround us. Taking the time to count our blessings helps us recognize God's hand in our lives.

Reflecting on the past year, think about the ways God has shown up for you. Perhaps He provided for a need, healed a relationship, or gave you strength during a challenging season. Remembering His faithfulness fills us with gratitude and gives us confidence for the future.

When we focus on what God has done, we're reminded that He is faithful and His love never changes. Let this week be a time of joyful remembrance and thanksgiving.

- Write down three specific ways you've seen God's faithfulness this year. Share these with a friend or family member to encourage them as well.

Prayer

Lord, thank You for Your faithfulness throughout this year. Help me to see Your blessings clearly and give You the glory for all You have done. Amen.

December 16

Gratitude in the Small Things

"Give thanks in all circumstances; for this is God's will for you in Christ Jesus."
1 Thessalonians 5:18

Gratitude isn't just about the big blessings; it's also about noticing the small, everyday gifts God provides. The warmth of a sunrise, the laughter of loved ones, or even the strength to face a new day are all reasons to give thanks.

In a fast-paced world, it's easy to overlook these small blessings. However, taking the time to slow down and appreciate them helps cultivate a heart of gratitude. When we give thanks in all circumstances, even in the hard times, we honor God and acknowledge His presence in every moment of our lives.

As you reflect on this year, look for the little ways God has blessed you. These seemingly small gifts are reminders of His constant care and attention to detail.

- Start a gratitude journal for the week. Each day, write down at least five small blessings you've experienced.

Prayer

Father, thank You for the countless small ways You bless me every day. Teach me to see Your goodness in every moment and to give thanks in all circumstances. Amen.

December 17
Lessons from the Valleys
"And we know that in all things God works for the good of those who love Him,
who have been called according to His purpose."
Romans 8:28

Life isn't always easy, and the past year may have included moments of difficulty and pain. However, even in the valleys, God is at work. He uses trials to refine us, strengthen our faith, and draw us closer to Him.

Reflecting on the challenges of this year, consider the lessons God has taught you. Perhaps He has shown you the importance of trusting Him, taught you patience, or deepened your compassion for others. These lessons, though often learned through hardship, are blessings that shape us into the people God wants us to be.

Instead of dwelling on what went wrong, thank God for how He has carried you through and used those moments for your growth. Trust that He is still working for your good.

- Write down one challenge you faced this year and the lesson or blessing you've gained from it. Pray for God to help you see His purpose in all circumstances.

Prayer
Lord, thank You for being with me in the valleys. Help me to see the blessings in the challenges and trust that You are always working for my good. Amen.

December 18
Celebrating Spiritual Growth
"But grow in the grace and knowledge of our Lord and Savior Jesus Christ. To
Him be glory both now and forever!"
2 Peter 3:18

Spiritual growth is one of the greatest blessings we can experience. As you reflect on this year, consider how your relationship with God has deepened. Have you grown in faith, prayer, or understanding of His Word? Even small steps forward are worth celebrating.

Growth often happens in ways we don't immediately notice. It might come through consistency in prayer, increased trust during hardships, or a newfound desire to serve others. Take time to thank God for how He has shaped you this year, knowing that He will continue to complete the good work He has started in you.

- Spend time reflecting on your spiritual journey this year. Write down areas where you've seen growth and areas where you'd like to continue growing.

Prayer

Lord, thank You for helping me grow in faith and grace this year. Continue to lead me closer to You and strengthen my walk with You in the coming year. Amen.

December 19

Honoring God with Your Blessings

"Every good and perfect gift is from above, coming down from the Father of the heavenly lights, who does not change like shifting shadows."

James 1:17

Every blessing we have is a gift from God. As we reflect on the past year, it's important to recognize that all good things come from Him. Honoring God with our blessings means using them to glorify Him and bless others.

Whether it's your time, talents, or resources, consider how you've stewarded what God has given you this year. Have you used your gifts to serve others and further God's kingdom? If not, ask Him to guide you in using your blessings for His glory in the coming year.

- Identify one blessing in your life that you can use to serve others. Make a plan to put it into action this week.

Prayer

Father, thank You for every blessing You have given me. Teach me to honor You by using my gifts to bless others and glorify Your name. Amen.

December 20
Thanking God for His Presence

"The Lord your God is with you, the Mighty Warrior who saves. He will take great delight in you; in His love, He will no longer rebuke you, but will rejoice over you with singing." Zephaniah 3:17

Above all blessings, the greatest gift we have is God's presence in our lives. His love, guidance, and peace are constant, even when everything else changes. Reflecting on the past year, remember the moments when you felt His presence the most.

God delights in you and rejoices over you. As you prepare for the new year, let the assurance of His presence fill you with peace and hope.

- Spend time in prayer today, simply thanking God for His presence in your life.

Prayer

Lord, thank You for being with me every step of the way this year. Your presence is my greatest blessing, and I praise You for never leaving or forsaking me. Amen.

December 21
Looking Ahead with Gratitude

"Give thanks to the Lord, for He is good; His love endures forever."
Psalm 107:1

As you end this year and prepare for the next, let gratitude fill your heart. God's goodness and love have carried you through, and His promises remain true for the future.

Looking ahead with gratitude doesn't mean knowing exactly what the future holds, but it does mean trusting the One who holds it. Let the lessons and blessings of this year give you confidence as you step into the new year.

• Write a prayer of thanksgiving for the past year and a prayer of surrender for the year ahead.

Prayer

Lord, I thank You for Your goodness and love this year. As I enter the new year, I surrender my plans to You and trust in Your faithfulness. Amen.

48

Renewing Hope for the Year Ahead

December 22
Anchoring Your Hope in God
"But those who hope in the Lord will renew their strength. They will soar on wings like eagles; they will run and not grow weary, they will walk and not be faint."
Isaiah 40:31

As the year ends, it's a perfect time to reflect on where your hope lies. While the world encourages us to pin our hopes on circumstances, achievements, or resolutions, God reminds us that true hope comes from Him. He is unchanging, faithful, and powerful, offering a hope that never fails.

When you anchor your hope in God, you are freed from the uncertainties of life. Whether the year ahead brings challenges or victories, you can trust that God will renew your strength and guide you. Look back at moments when He carried you this year, and let those memories remind you that He will continue to be your refuge.

As you step into a new year, commit to placing your trust in God rather than fleeting things. His plans are good, His promises are true, and His love is steadfast.

- Spend time in prayer, surrendering your hopes and dreams for the new year to God. Write down a scripture or promise that you want to focus on throughout the year.

Prayer

Lord, as I look to the year ahead, help me anchor my hope in You. Renew my strength and guide my steps as I trust in Your plans. Amen.

December 23

Trusting God with Your Future

"For I know the plans I have for you," declares the Lord, "plans to prosper you and not to harm you, plans to give you hope and a future."

Jeremiah 29:11

The uncertainty of the future can sometimes feel overwhelming. But as a child of God, you have the assurance that your future is secure in His hands. God's plans for you are filled with hope and purpose, even when they don't align with your expectations.

This scripture reminds us that God's plans are always for our good, even when we can't see the full picture. Trusting Him with your future means surrendering control and believing that His ways are higher than ours. It also means letting go of worry and embracing the peace that comes from knowing that God is in charge.

As you prepare for the new year, take a moment to surrender your plans and desires to God. Trust that He will guide you, provide for you, and fulfill His promises in His perfect timing.

- Write down one area of your life where you need to trust God more with the future. Pray specifically for His guidance and peace in that area.

Prayer

Father, I trust You with my future. Help me to surrender my plans and dreams to You, knowing that Your ways are higher and Your plans are perfect. Amen.

December 24

Leaving the Past Behind

"Forget the former things; do not dwell on the past. See, I am doing a new thing!
Now it springs up; do you not perceive it?"
Isaiah 43:18-19

As you prepare for the year ahead, it's important to leave behind the things that no longer serve God's purpose in your life. This might mean letting go of past mistakes, failures, or disappointments. Holding onto the past can weigh you down, but trusting God to do a new thing brings freedom and hope.

God is always at work, creating new opportunities for growth and blessing. By focusing on His promises, you can embrace the fresh start He offers. This doesn't mean ignoring the lessons of the past, but rather allowing them to shape your future in positive ways.

Let this be a year where you fully embrace the new things God is doing in your life. Trust Him to lead you into His plans with hope and confidence.

- Take time to write down anything you feel you need to leave behind as you enter the new year. Ask God for strength and grace to release it fully.

Prayer

Lord, help me to let go of the past and embrace the new things You are doing in my life. Thank You for Your promise of hope and renewal. Amen.

December 25

Setting God-Centered Goals

"Commit to the Lord whatever you do, and He will establish your plans."
Proverbs 16:3

The start of a new year is often a time for setting goals and making resolutions. However, goals rooted in God's will have eternal value. When you seek His guidance and commit your plans to Him, He aligns your desires with His purpose.

God-centered goals focus on spiritual growth, serving others, and living out your faith. These goals might include deepening your prayer life, serving in your community, or sharing God's love with those around you. Setting these kinds of goals allows you to partner with God in the work He is doing in your life and the world.

As you reflect on the year ahead, ask God to reveal the goals He wants you to pursue. Trust Him to equip you with everything you need to fulfill them.

- Spend time in prayer, asking God to guide you in setting goals for the new year. Write down one spiritual goal you feel led to pursue.

Prayer

Lord, I commit my goals and plans for the new year to You. Guide me in setting goals that align with Your will and bring glory to Your name. Amen.

December 26

Renewing Your Mind

"Do not conform to the pattern of this world, but be transformed by the renewing of your mind."
Romans 12:2

A new year is a perfect opportunity to renew your mind and align your thoughts with God's truth. The world's patterns often lead to worry, comparison, and discontentment, but God's Word offers peace, joy, and purpose.

Renewing your mind involves filling it with God's promises and letting His truth shape your perspective. This daily renewal empowers you to face challenges with faith and make decisions that honor Him.

As you step into the new year, commit to spending time in God's Word. Allow His truth to transform your mind and guide your actions.

- Create a plan for daily Bible reading or devotional time in the new year. Start with a passage or topic that encourages renewal and growth.

Prayer

Father, renew my mind with Your truth. Help me to focus on Your promises and align my thoughts with Your will as I enter this new year. Amen.